MW00909956

GOD AND HEALING OF THE MIND

Printed by Print Solutions Partnership, Wallington, England

Published by Crossbridge Books
345 Old Birmingham Road
Bromsgrove B60 1NX
Tel: 0121 447 7897

Copyright © 2006 by Crossbridge Books.

All rights reserved. No part of this publication may be
reproduced, stored in a retrieval system, or transmitted
by any means – electronic, mechanical, photocopying,
recording or otherwise – without prior permission of
the Copyright owner.

ISBN: 0 9549708 2 9
British Library Cataloguing in Publication Data.
A catalogue record for this book is available from the
British Library.

Revised edition 2006.
First published in 1983 by Bridge Publishing, Inc.

All Biblical quotations are taken from the Revised Standard
Version of the Bible unless otherwise noted as the King James
Version (KJV) or the Living Bible (TLB).

GOD AND HEALING
OF THE MIND
A Spiritual Guide to Mental Health

TREVOR DEARING

CROSSBRIDGE BOOKS

Sight, riches, *healing* of *the mind;*
Yea, all I need in Thee to find
O Lamb of God, I come, I come.

(Charlotte Elliott)

ACKNOWLEDGEMENTS

I am indebted to many people for the thoughts and experiences that have gone into the writing of this book. This applies particularly to those many people who, by seeking my help, have allowed me to enter deeply into their lives and thereby enabled me to fathom how the grace of God can reach inner sicknesses and so heal the soul. I want to thank them for the privilege they have accorded me and for the way in which they have helped my ministry to develop. Further, I could not have found the time, due to my ministerial duties, to commit my thoughts to print without the dedicated help of Enid Holt as my typist and Heather McClay as my discerning and constructive critic. I would also like to express my gratitude to my wife, Anne, with whom all my thoughts have been thoroughly discussed, and who has been my constant helper and companion in the ministry of inner healing.

PREFACE

This book is about inner healing; that is, the healing of the soul. However, because the Bible teaches that the "soul" is made up of the mind, the emotions and the will, this book can be described as *a spiritual guide to mental health*. It describes the fundamental teaching of the Bible about how the loving, healing grace of God reaches our inner being in order continually to restore us to harmony, peace and joy. It shows that God's purpose is to make men and women whole, and that His work of salvation involves the mind as well as the spirit of man, and that suffering people can therefore confidently expect Him to heal them.

Throughout this book I have assumed that readers experiencing serious mental breakdown have sought medical help. However, all my experience, both personal and through counselling others, has proven to me that because human beings have spirits as well as minds and bodies, there exists within each of us also, in addition to the medical approach, a spiritual gateway through which God's healing can flow into the depths of our beings. I hope therefore that readers will be able to grasp easily the spiritual principles set out in each chapter and that, as they follow the counsel which is given, they will soon be experiencing God's grace at work within them, bringing them into new realms of spiritual and mental health.

CONTENTS

1 INTRODUCTION

I was nineteen years of age when I first sat in a church and pleaded with God to help me. For eight years I had endured the agony of desperate fear and deep depression, and now I felt I had reached the end of my tether. I just couldn't go on any longer.

My life had been one of prolonged absences from school, followed by frequent changes in employment. Since the beginning of my illness, every night had been interminable and sleepless while I lay trembling in bed, shaking and perspiring with fear, feeling that I was falling ever deeper into an endless, bottomless pit. Days proved little better than nights because I lived in terror of going insane, dying, or even worse, of being buried alive. Consequently, I was always weak, "washed out", and even afraid to venture into the streets because of the sheer panic I knew would always grip me. I also suffered from an intense depression, which shrouded my mind like a heavy, black curtain. Everything and everyone seemed to be unreal and far away. I went from one obsession to another, and at one time I was convinced that if I didn't get into bed before ten o'clock I would die!

No one seemed to understand me. My doctor described my condition as "chronic depression", "hysteria" and a "severe anxiety state" on medical certificates, which also stated that my father's presence was "urgently needed at home". I suffered from many delusions and for a period even became convinced that everyone, including my parents and the doctor, had formed a conspiracy to poison me. I went berserk and, in the end, desperately contemplated suicide, only to discover I was even more terrified of

1

dying than I was of living! I was trapped! There was no way out!

The doctor suggested that I should see a psychiatrist, but my parents resisted the idea, for in those days there was a real fear and stigma attached to being admitted to what were then called "lunatic asylums". I was eventually given drug therapy at home, which made my life a little more tolerable. I was, however, still a very sick young man when I sat in Queen's Hall Methodist Church in the city of Hull, and, in sheer desperation, cried out, "God, help me!"

Something happened! The words ringing in my mind were those of the sermon being preached that night by Rev. William D. Watts, the minister. He constantly reiterated the words of Jesus, "Come to me, all who labour and are heavy laden, and I will give you rest. Take my yoke upon you, and learn from me; for I am gentle and lowly in heart, and you will find rest for your souls. For my yoke is easy, and my burden is light" (Matt. 11:28-30). In these moments Jesus seemed actually to be standing in front of me and to be speaking directly to me!

I became very excited. I felt there was hope for me at last! I was actually going to receive God's help to make me well. *He* could and would, I was sure, enable me to live a useful, happy life. I couldn't at that moment in time see just how He was going to do it, but a deep peace began immediately to fill my whole being. I knew that God was all-powerful, that He was real, and, further, that He was interested in me. What more could I want? Light flashed into my darkness. Hope chased away my despair. I was being healed!

In the months that followed I drew ever closer to God and felt a deep sense of destiny over my life. I still had a long way to go to a complete cure, and I was to discover that the Lord's method of healing me would not, in any way, be instantaneous or magical. The maxim "God helps those who help themselves" was certainly going to prove true for me, as with His help I fought battle after battle and gained ground in health in a step-by-step process. Even while I was being healed I had periods when I felt I was slipping back into sickness as depression again enveloped me or panic gripped me, but eventually I would always experience that underneath me were His everlasting arms (Deut. 33:27*)*. Through the healing process I learned so much of eternal value, lessons which, despite the pain, I would not like to have missed.

I had known some periods of remission before my conversion, but during them I had always felt I was sitting on a barrel of dynamite that might explode at any time! Now there was a difference, because with God as my helper I was confident my healing would be *permanent and complete.* My hope was not to prove unfounded!

Soon after my discovery of God's great love I began to read books about psychology and eventually decided that I would see a psychiatrist for a check-up. He assured me I was well on the way to full health and seemed to wish that all his patients could discover my source of divine help. After three visits he declared I had no need to see him again and predicted that my newly found mental and emotional health would continue for the rest of my life. Despite minor setbacks in times of excess stress, strain and exhaustion and an exacting Christian ministry, his prognosis has proved to be excitingly true.

Much to my joy I soon discovered I was also being healed of the many physical disorders which had earlier been caused or aggravated by my mental condition. I began to walk upright instead of with a stoop, and my thin frame began to fill out as it was clothed with new flesh. My heart, which had been rapidly beating itself to death, became normal, and other weak organs regained strength; my skin, once covered with boils, gave way to new, unmarked flesh. Even bald patches on my head began to disappear! God was making me a whole person in body, mind and spirit.

Eventually, I entered theological college and discovered that God had so wonderfully healed my disorientated mind that I was able to obtain a degree in theology and eventually marry a pretty and vivacious nurse named Anne, who has always supported me and shared my ministry to the full. So it was as a completely well and happy man that I embarked upon my Christian ministry, first in the Methodist Church and then as an ordained minister of the Church of England.

On May 10, 1969, God brought me into an even deeper experience of the power of His Spirit and anointed me for an evangelistic and healing ministry. So, a young man who once was too frightened even to go to the end of the street has now travelled to the far corners of the earth to proclaim "release to the captives, ... to set at liberty those who are oppressed" (Luke 4:18) and minister God's healing power to many thousands of mentally and physically sick people.

The way has not always been easy, but God has helped me to live a life that has been useful beyond anything I had once dared to hope or expect. I have proved Jesus' words to be true—"All things are possible to him who believes" (Mark 9:23).

So, I am addressing this book to all who have needs similar to those which once crippled and nearly ruined my life. I want to share with them the truths that God has imparted to me on my pilgrimage from sickness to health. I am certain that it is God's will to heal all who respond at depth to His love as revealed to us in His Word, the Bible.

I shall also draw a great deal on the insights I have gained from counselling many needy people. It is my hope that the teaching and advice given will prove helpful to those engaged in a similar ministry to the ever-increasing number of people in the world today who need deep, inner, emotional healing.

2 HOW TO RECOGNISE THE NEED FOR INNER HEALING

Since the time God brought me out of deep emotional illness into a new, happy and useful life, it has been my privilege to help scores of people to a new wholeness by teaching them how to open their lives to the power of God's love. In order to do this, however, I had first to learn how to recognise the many ways in which the need for inner healing expresses itself. This is possible because our minds as well as our bodies have built-in "need indicators"—real ways of telling us that something is very wrong deep down in our being. The most common of these symptoms are:

(1) *Constant over-aggressive, dominating, withdrawing, or attention-seeking behaviour.*
All these are, in one way or another, attempts by sufferers to cover up and compensate for deep feelings of rejection. Perhaps a soul-shattering experience occurred in their childhood or at some other time when they desperately needed love and security. They also indicate that the sufferers have received such inner wounds at the hands of others that they are terrified of exposing themselves emotionally to anyone ever again. It is for this reason that they either withdraw into a protective shell of non-communication or keep others at bay by aggressive behaviour.

(2) *Intense, abnormal fears,* for instance, of open spaces or spaces or of being in a confined space. Fears can attach themselves to almost anything—storms, cancer, death,

7

hurting others, insanity, travel or of being in strange places. Such fears at their worst can become sheer terror as the sufferer is gripped with uncontrollable panic.

(3) *Acute and chronic depression.* This can include a feeling of intense physical weariness and even the complete inability to get out of bed or to be able to go to work. To those who are in a state of depression, life seems meaningless and empty as the mind becomes increasingly preoccupied with morbid thoughts. At its deepest, it feels like a deep, dark dungeon in which one has been incarcerated for life. Those who are lost in depression are often completely unable to communicate with anyone. They may blame such things as their homes, the area in which they live, relatives, friends, religion, or even their appearance; the permutations are endless. It is important to realise, however, that these things *are not the real cause* of the trouble; *they are the symptoms* indicating that deep, inner healing is urgently needed.

(4) *Anxieties.* We all have reasonable and natural worries from time to time, but people who suffer from this form of mental pain are usually in a *perpetual* state of anxiety. They switch from one seemingly desperate concern to another, and the terrible panics into which they get are altogether out of proportion to their real problems. They seem to be unable to learn not to worry.

(5) *Obsessions.* If a person is by nature methodical, then deep emotional pain will often express itself in life-crippling obsessions about such things as dress, behaviour, cleanliness, religion, safety, turning off lights, locking doors, etc. Because living with a person suffering from these distressful symptoms can be very difficult, marital or other relationships frequently break down. The person tends to

feel desperately insecure and can even go berserk if his code of rules and regulations is not kept. I was once asked to help a young lady who was terribly obsessed about the appearance of her face. She spent countless hours and most of her income on facial creams and cleansing agents and was always in a state of anguish. All this was completely unnecessary, since she was in fact a very attractive young lady. People suffering from such obsessions are always unable to draw the line sensibly between genuine carefulness and abnormal, compulsive behaviour.

(6) *Insomnia.* This is a common accompaniment of mental pain. The mind, deep down, is so busy grappling with its problems that it just cannot rest. Efforts to go to sleep do nothing except keep the person awake, and the sufferer usually spends agonising nights extremely worried about how he will cope with life the next day.

(7) *Confusion.* When the pressures of life mount up to an intolerable level some insecure people cannot help caving in emotionally. They find they are totally unable to sort out their problems which, *to them,* have become of critical importance. Decision-making becomes impossible and the person eventually collapses helplessly into inactivity, panic and bewilderment. He finds he cannot cope and desperately seeks help in many real, or imaginary, circumstances. His phone bills mount up as he makes what he believes to be urgent calls to his friends, whose advice is rarely acted upon.

(8) *Delusions and hallucinations.* We now cross a borderline in our consideration of the different forms of mental suffering. In all the conditions I have so far described, the person is acutely aware of being in need of help, in some form or another. The difficulty in treating

9

people suffering from delusions and hallucinations, however, is that they are usually convinced that their experience is real, and that everyone who disagrees with them is wrong. Some are convinced that many people are plotting their downfall, or that neighbours are getting at them; others are sure that the rays of the sun or other invisible forces are destroying them. These people are described by the medical profession as paranoid. Another form of delusion is that of hearing voices, which swear, blaspheme or impel the person to perform certain actions, or go to particular places. I have known people who have actually been urged to kill by the voices that tormented them.

Another common form of delusion is that of grandeur when the sufferer is sure that he is a very important person, like Jesus, Mohammed or a prophet, who has come to announce the end of the age. Delusions, however, can take many forms, even to that of believing one's faithful partner is having adulterous affairs with others. Audible hallucinations often accompanied by those of a visual nature occur as the patient, unable to cope with reality, retreats into a world of his own from which he is deeply afraid to emerge.

(9) *Religious delusions.* When a mentally sick person is of a spiritual disposition, then his illness can take on a religious form. I have found such people often seek the help of *many* ministers and priests, but despite the fact that they receive rational answers to their questions, they still continue to be as troubled as ever. So Christians suffering from chronic anxiety have come to my office to describe in agonising detail their many desperate religious problems and doubts. Some, in a condition of chronic depression, have become morbidly preoccupied with the thought of having disobeyed God, or that they have committed the

"unforgivable sin". Some think the voices they are hearing are those of demonic powers, while others think that God Himself is saying what are obviously bizarre things to them. So, any who try to help such people must first ascertain whether they are dealing with a genuinely rational religious problem or whether, in fact, the person's problems are an expression of deeper underlying mental pain. If the problems are genuine, then the enquirer will readily accept rational answers to his questions. If, however, the person is mentally sick, such answers will make no contribution at all to a solution until the person's *real* deep problems have been uncovered.

(10) *Possession.* Sometimes mental pain and suffering can so distort one's thinking that what is normally a healthy human activity, such as religion or sex, becomes completely out of the person's control and adversely affects the whole of his life. The person begins to engage in extravagant behaviour, which can cause considerable embarrassment and even harm to others. Once again, the counsellor must know how to recognise the difference between genuine, normal behaviour and its pathological counterpart, such as religious or sex mania. Normal behaviour in these realms should lead to happiness, while that caused by deep-seated emotional disorientation will only increase misery and distress.

I am convinced that due to the pressures of our permissive society an increasing number of people are entering into conditions of emotional derangement because of their constant, wilful, excessive, sinful behaviour or by engaging in abnormal spiritistic activities that are prohibited by the Bible (Deut. 18:10-12). So, for instance, people who deliberately, wholeheartedly, and frequently give themselves to acts of sexual perversion begin to find that such behaviour eventually *controls them* and people who engage in occult activities often find themselves literally taken over and controlled by these spiritual forces. These activities have in fact been banned by God, because He has always known the disastrous effects they will have upon our souls and spirits. Keen discernment and practical knowledge, however, is needed to differentiate between such cases of *possession* and other forms of mental suffering. I have found that in genuine cases of possession, the onset of the symptoms has nearly always coincided with involvement either in the occult or in flagrant sin. This is a religious problem with spiritual as well as psychological symptoms, which, thank God, has an answer in the victory of Christ over all evil forces. It has been my privilege and responsibility to bring deliverance to many possessed people. In my experience a simple act of deliverance (exorcism) has often saved them from perhaps many years of fruitless medical treatment. Usually, ministry for the healing of the mind must follow exorcism ministry, in order that the shocks, bruises, hurts, painful memories and other emotional problems caused by the condition* may be dealt with.

(11)   *Physical symptoms.*   In many cases of apparent physical disorders, there can be deep-seated mental and emotional unrest, which needs to be recognised and faced up to in order for the sufferer really to become a whole person.   Doctors have told me it is certain that many common illnesses such as migraine headaches, allergies, digestive and spinal problems, and sinusitis can be caused or intensified by underlying emotional causes. Certainly our mental well-being *does* affect our physical health and that is why the Bible states that God wishes to do more than heal us; His intention is to make us *whole;* in body, soul

*For a detailed study, see my book *Supernatural Superpowers,* Logos International.

12

and spirit.

(12)   *Addictions.* It is obvious that when a person is
mentally well he will certainly be free from addictions to
alcohol, drugs and compulsive eating, or its opposite—
anorexia nervosa, which leads to malnutrition and
starvation. Such addictions are usually desperate attempts
to escape from unbearable mental pain. The underlying
mental problem must be uncovered, faced, and dealt with in
order for the person to be completely free.

It is very interesting to see that Jesus Christ spoke
about the needs of those suffering deep inner pain and
sickness at the very outset of His ministry (Luke 4:18). He
used the words "bruised", "broken-hearted" and "captives"
to describe these conditions. Jesus described as
"prisoners" all those who had become deranged through
possession by evil spiritual forces through involvement in
occultism, addictions or constant wilful sin. He said He
had come to set such people free, free to be themselves,
free to love and to be loved. Similarly, an essential part of
His mission was to set at liberty those who were "bruised.".
Thus, His message and ministry were to be addressed to all
whose lives had been seriously hurt and damaged by the
words and actions of others or their own reactions to the
circumstances of their lives.

The Gospel of Jesus Christ therefore was and still is
for the whole person, bringing a spiritual answer to the
needs even of the broken-hearted, those whose whole
personality, their very self, has been smashed and dis-
integrated by the pressure of life and circumstances. Jesus
himself recognises and answers all the needs of mind and
heart.

I must emphasise that this brief chapter is only meant to
be an outline study of some of the most common forms of

mental suffering, which are important for both counsellors and sufferers to recognise and face. When I was in a condition of fear, panic, anxiety and depression, my first real step to healing came when I was told by my doctor that I was as genuinely sick as a person suffering from any form of physical illness. It was a real relief to know that I couldn't be expected simply to "pull myself together" as some expected. I realised that my "odd" feelings and sensations, as well as my terrible fears and depressions, were being endured by many other people as well as myself, and that the medical profession and others were seeking the answers to this ever-growing problem. A further dynamic release came when I saw that God knew and understood all about such problems and had provided a supernatural answer to them.

3   GOD AND THE SUFFERING MIND

Those who are suffering deep mental pain can be sure their condition is certainly not God's will.   Generally speaking, two factors work together to produce deep emotional sicknesses.   The first is the person's own temperament; the second is the accumulation of events that take place in and around his life.   Neither of them is the direct result of anything done by God.   Many people are, naturally, very sensitive; they were born with a tendency to feel deeply, be easily hurt, concerned, introspective, analytical and even to be anxious and fearful.   This is the sort of person they always have been and always will be, whether they like it or not, and so it is best for them to accept themselves as they are, and thank God for the many good and positive results that come from having such a disposition—for instance, they will always tend to be loving, sympathetic and kind.

I have always had to face up to having a very "nervous" temperament.   I can never remember a period in my childhood when I wasn't analysing the meaning and purpose of my life and feeling rather insecure in the world around me.   I had a brother and two sisters who shared the same upbringing as myself, yet I was the only one in the family who eventually broke down emotionally.   My relatives always seemed to cope with the stresses of life far better than I was ever able to.   This was because I was much more predisposed towards mental breakdown as a result of my extremely sensitive nature.

Emotional sicknesses, however, are not only caused by people's temperaments.   Very few people actually break down until they have to face situations of unbearable stress or endure terrible shocks, which come to them from outside of themselves. Thus, for example, pressures exerted by parents, teachers or other superiors upon a sensitive, insecure person may become so intense that he will begin to cave in emotionally and begin to manifest symptoms of deep mental pain. Rejection by parents or friends, marital disharmony, failure, guilt, unemployment, bereavement, illness, an operation, a miscarriage, and many other unavoidable events in life can become external causes of a person becoming emotionally sick.

In the majority of cases, therefore, mental illness is caused by the interaction of what the Bible calls the world (the imperfect environment around us) and the flesh (our imperfect, fallen human nature within us). It must be remembered that individuals respond very differently to the circumstances of their lives, which vary greatly for each one of us. In the process some people become emotionally bruised and broken while others become severely mentally sick. *This is not a condition God ever wants for His children.* We can be certain that despite the fact that we live in a fallen world, God wants us to be victorious, secure, free, well and happy through a deep relationship with Him.

It is outside the scope of this book to investigate why God allows our fallen nature and this imperfect world to go on as it does.*

However, we can be sure that it is God's perfect will for all of us to be perfectly and completely *whole,* in body, soul and spirit. It is of paramount importance for our mental health that we truly comprehend that despite how we sometimes feel, *God is love* (1 John 4:8). Our picture of what God is like is very important for our mental

---

*For a brief study of this matter see my book *Supernatural Healing Today* (Logos International). For a deeper study see C.S. Lewis's *The Problem* of *Pain* (Fontana Books).

health.

It was for this reason that I once asked a class of teenagers at school to describe their impression of God. Most of them returned to me a blank sheet of paper! This is because they recognised that God is *beyond* our highest thoughts and imaginings. He is more vast even than the universe He created. He is more powerful than all the combined forces and sources of energy that we can know. God is without beginning and without end, inhabiting another dimension, beyond all time and space. The Bible puts this in the words: "For my thoughts are not your thoughts, neither are your ways my ways, says the Lord. For as the heavens are higher than the earth, so are my ways higher than your ways and my thoughts than your thoughts" (Isa. 55:8-9). It says that before Him all the nations are "like a drop from a bucket" (Isa. 40:15) and men appear like "grasshoppers" (Isa. 40:22). Also, the reason why my class of teenagers found it difficult to describe God was that He is Spirit and therefore not available to our senses; we can neither see, touch nor hear Him in any normal way.

The Christian Gospel (or Good News), however, is that *God has made himself known* to mankind—the creatures whom He has made in His own image, the crown of His creation. *Christians* know that God himself came among men and women through His Son, Jesus Christ; that Jesus is "the image of the invisible God" (Col. 1:15). "For in him the whole fulness of deity dwells bodily" (Col. 2:9). He even once said, "He who has seen me has seen the Father" (John 14:9). This means that every word Jesus ever spoke echoes the voice of God, and every deed He ever performed was an act of God. *Jesus shows God's nature, and in Him we can see what God is really like in His attitude towards us.* When Jesus went about healing every disease and every infirmity

17

among the people (Matt. 4:23), He forever demonstrated that God's will is to heal all who come to Him in faith.

God's will for us all, therefore, is that we should be well, in body, *mind* and spirit and we can be *sure* that the power of His love is always directed towards that end. As early as the days of the Old Testament, in proclaiming God's Word a prophet said, "Thou dost keep him in *perfect peace,* whose mind is stayed on Thee, because he trusts in Thee" (Isa. 26:3). Later, Jesus clearly demonstrated God's loving will and power when He drove disturbing and evil forces from people's lives (Matt. 8:16). Towards the end of His ministry He actually bequeathed His peace to mankind in the words, "Peace I leave with you; my peace I give to you; let not your hearts be troubled, neither let them be afraid" (John 14:27). Above all, He even laid down His life to carry our sorrows and in order to make us whole (Isa. 53:4-6, John 10:15). All who read the Bible should understand that the frequently recurring phrase, "to be saved", means literally *"to be made whole and healthy"*. St. Paul therefore admirably summed up God's entire purpose for us when He said that Jesus will present us before His Father's throne sound in body, soul and spirit. Paul was so confident that this purpose would one day be fulfilled that he declared: "He who calls you is faithful, and he will do it" (1 Thess. 5:24; see also Jude 24).

Sadly, I have met scores of people whose whole lives have been made unhappy because they have been indoctrinated with warped and distorted ideas about God. They have been brought up in rigid, puritanical homes and churches where God has been presented to them as a tyrant, seemingly just waiting for their next act of disobedience, in order to punish them and send them to hell. These unfortunate people have also been taught to be *very* introspective about their sins and to have extremely negative views about many harmless pleasures of life.

Sadly, some might have been much more happy had they been brought up as pagans, because they have been indoctrinated in *religiosity* in which God has always to be appeased, rather than *Christianity* wherein He is received as a loving Saviour. Wrong religion is always conducive to emotional stress, guilt problems, and mental breakdowns. However, when the truth is grasped that *God is love, that His very essence and nature is love,* that He cares, knows all about us and loves us just the same; when we see that He comes to us just *where we are,* with an offer of healing love (Luke 10:33) and is always a very present help in time of need (Ps. 46:1), then we are in a position to be truly liberated from all that hurts us. As we learn how better to respond to His love, to get to know Him, talk to Him and trust Him, we find that in His presence is fullness of joy and at His right hand there are pleasures for evermore (Ps. 16:11).

4 GOD'S GATEWAY FOR HEALING .

God *wants* us to be well because He is our Father, and He *is able* to make us well because we are made in His image. The Bible teaches us that there is a basic, fundamental likeness between every human being and the Being of God, and that as the children of God we share the very nature of our heavenly Father. This means that because God is spirit (John 4:24), we also are spiritual beings, and it is through our spirit that we are able to have deep communion with God. It is through our spirit that He is able to flood us with His healing love.

The way in which God's healing reaches us is often described in such words as:

> He touched me, oh, He touched me
> And oh, the joy that floods my soul;
> Something happened, and now I know
> He touched me and made me whole.
>
> (W.T. Gaither)

or

> Just as I am, poor, wretched, blind;
> Sight, riches, *healing of the mind,*
> Yea, all I need in Thee to find,
> O Lamb of God, I come, I come.
>
> (Charlotte Elliott)

These raise the question, however, about just how God can actually touch us in order to heal us in the depths of our beings.

A simple diagram will help to explain how He in fact does this. It portrays the way in which God has made every one of us to function as human beings, and therefore as His children.

This diagram (A) portrays the biblical teaching that the inner core of our being is our spirit, and that this is closely related to what the Bible calls our soul. In the Bible's view of man's nature, the soul is comprised of our mind (thinking ability), emotions (feelings) and our will (determination). The spirit and the soul are both invisible and therefore spiritual. The visible, physical part of us is our body—some of which can be seen when you look in a mirror; the rest can be photographed by X-rays. It is the agent through which you engage in two-way traffic with the world outside you. Through it, you turn your thoughts and feelings into actions, and, by means of its senses (hearing, seeing, touching, etc.), impressions from the world are fed back into your being.

Further, it is very important for our study that we see that what goes on in one part of our being inevitably affects the other parts. In the diagram this is shown by the direction of the arrows. So, for instance, when we are insecure and frightened (in the soul area), then our heart beats much more quickly (in the body area). In a similar way if we are *physically* sick, we often feel *emotionally* down and depressed. A human being is not simply a complicated piece of machinery, like a car engine; he thinks, feels and wills (James 1:4). He is an organic, integrated fusion of spirit, soul and body, each part of which affects the well-being of the other.

Doctors make use of this fact whenever they give drugs to a person who is suffering from mental illness. They know that certain chemicals definitely affect the working of certain parts of the brain, which, in turn, have a tranquillising or uplifting influence upon the mind. In this way they seek to reduce the distress of the mind through the gateway of the body.

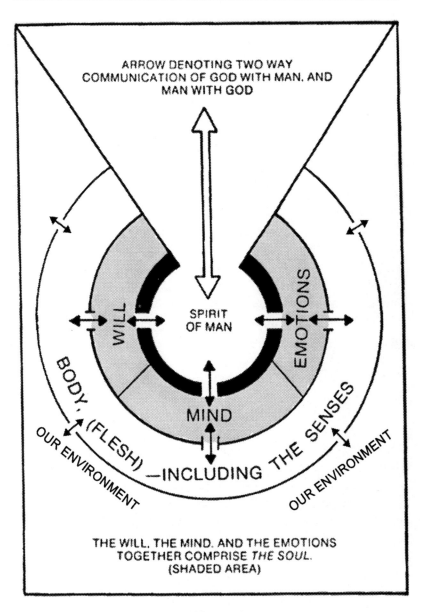

ARROW DENOTING TWO WAY COMMUNICATION OF GOD WITH MAN, AND MAN WITH GOD

SPIRIT OF MAN

WILL

EMOTIONS

MIND

BODY, (FLESH) —INCLUDING THE SENSES

OUR ENVIRONMENT

OUR ENVIRONMENT

THE WILL, THE MIND, AND THE EMOTIONS TOGETHER COMPRISE *THE SOUL.* (SHADED AREA)

DIAGRAM A.

Psychiatrists also usually prescribe drugs or other useful physical methods to help emotionally disturbed people. Such methods are constantly changing and advancing and, at its best, psychiatric treatment should never be scorned by Christians, because it is part of God's healing programme to alleviate the suffering of mankind. Good psychiatrists seek to probe into the mind, or soul area of the patient's life, to try to uncover the *real* causes of their troubles rather than merely seeking to subdue the symptoms. Today they tend to use also group therapy to bring people's hidden problems out into the open. Certainly, I was helped a great deal by a sympathetic psychiatrist, with whom I could honestly and confidentially discuss my confusions and perplexities. I am sure that God was present at these interviews, seeking to help me through someone who understood the workings of the mind.

From the diagram of the biblical picture of man's being, however, we see that there is another gateway of healing besides that of the body (the field of the doctor), and that of the mind (the field of the psychiatrist); it is *the gateway of the spirit*. It is the gateway *especially* used by God for His all-powerful love to saturate and reach *every* area of His children's lives and beings. When there is a beautiful, restored relationship between a person and God, then His divine healing can flow into the spirit, and there is *literally* no limit to the good things that can happen in a person's spirit, soul and body. Jesus specifically commissioned and empowered His people to preach this Good News, which is that God's desire is to save and to heal all mankind (Luke 9:1; 10:9). In the past, the healing aspects of this ministry have been sadly overlooked; but now, all over the world, it is being rediscovered and used to bring God's answer to the ever-increasing volume of mental and physical illness in today's society.

Christians, while affirming the fact that the medical profession has a real place in God's healing programme, must also strongly proclaim the possibility of divine healing through the gateway of the human spirit. Christians can confidently assert both from the truths of the Bible and the evidence of their experience that God is ready and willing to heal the shattered minds of those who come to Him in faith.

5 GOD AND THE DEPTHS
OF OUR BEING

It is important for our inner healing that we see that God has provided a gateway through which He can enter into the very depths of our being, but we must also understand just what it is that He has to do within us in order to set us free from such things as fears, obsessions, depression, tensions, insomnia, anxiety and delusions. Once a sufferer has seen the way in which God works, he will be fully able to cooperate with God in His healing work. *Divine healing is not magical.* Because God gave us freedom of will, He depends upon *our* response to His love, our opening up ourselves to Him, and our determined efforts based upon faith in Him, in order to heal us. As the Bible says, "... work out your own salvation ... for God is at work in you, both to will and to work for his good pleasure" (Phil. 2:12-13).

I can well remember how much a book by the late Methodist minister, Dr Leslie Weatherhead,* helped the process of God's healing in my life. For years I had lived in fear and dread, feeling different and peculiar, without even beginning to understand what was the matter with me. The insights gained from his book were like a great beam of light which illumined my condition, and built up my faith in God's power to heal me.

This was because, following the reading of this book, I no longer had to rely on blind faith, for I had begun to understand the healing process God would use to bring me health and happiness. From my experience in counselling,

---
* *Psychology and Life*

27

with many people suffering from mental pain, I know that inner healing takes a gigantic step forward when they gain similar enlightenment. Once again a diagram (B) will help. It portrays in more detail the soul, or what today is more frequently called the mind area, of our beings.

From this picture we can see that, like an iceberg, the conscious area is only the tip of the mind. It consists of what we are thinking, feeling and endeavouring to do right at this moment. Underneath this in the subconscious are the memories, hopes, fears, feelings and thoughts which we can easily recall. Still further below these in the unconscious area are the emotions attached to events that are even more difficult to remember, and also those which go right back to the very time before we were born, which we cannot remember at all.

It is extremely important to realise that all emotions in both the subconscious and the unconscious are still affecting our lives. They are making a real impression right now upon our minds. Like "bubbling springs" they continually send up all sorts of pleasant or very unpleasant feelings in the direction of our conscious minds. All of us, from our earliest days, without realising it, push strong, frightening feelings deep down into that unconscious area of the mind because they are too painful for us consciously to cope with. We do just the same to all the terrible emotions surrounding shocks, guilt, failure, rejection, insecurity, and other traumatic experiences.

It is my firm belief, based on the teaching of Jesus, and on my experience in healing ministry, that *evil spiritual* forces are also able to send dreadful feelings through the spirit area of our beings, up into the conscious mind. This experience is what we call spiritual *oppression*. The further, and more dreadful state, of *possession* occurs when these entities actually take up lodging in the spirit and dominate the whole of a person's life.

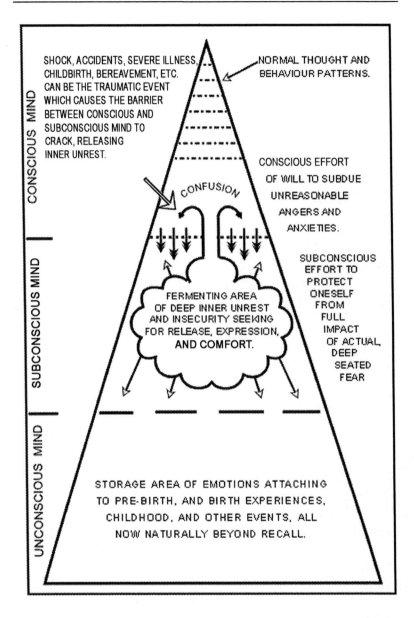

CONSCIOUS MIND

SUBCONSCIOUS MIND

UNCONSCIOUS MIND

SHOCK, ACCIDENTS, SEVERE ILLNESS, CHILDBIRTH, BEREAVEMENT, ETC. CAN BE THE TRAUMATIC EVENT WHICH CAUSES THE BARRIER BETWEEN CONSCIOUS AND SUBCONSCIOUS MIND TO CRACK, RELEASING INNER UNREST.

NORMAL THOUGHT AND BEHAVIOUR PATTERNS.

CONFUSION

CONSCIOUS EFFORT OF WILL TO SUBDUE UNREASONABLE ANGERS AND ANXIETIES.

SUBCONSCIOUS EFFORT TO PROTECT ONESELF FROM FULL IMPACT OF ACTUAL, DEEP SEATED FEAR

FERMENTING AREA OF DEEP INNER UNREST AND INSECURITY SEEKING FOR RELEASE, EXPRESSION, AND COMFORT.

STORAGE AREA OF EMOTIONS ATTACHING TO PRE-BIRTH, AND BIRTH EXPERIENCES, CHILDHOOD, AND OTHER EVENTS, ALL NOW NATURALLY BEYOND RECALL.

DIAGRAM B

This means that although we "feel" mental pain in the conscious area of our minds, its cause really lies much deeper down in the subconscious, unconscious, or spirit parts of our being. The conscious pain we feel is a symptom of some deeper emotional, or spiritual problem, which is too terrifying for us to face, or which many people are not even aware that they have within them. Let us look at some examples.

Mrs A came to see me, stating that she was having a nervous breakdown. She was chronically depressed and spent most of her days in bed. After a lot of counselling she began to see that her feeling of depression was a symptom of much deeper problems with which she could not cope. Her feelings of total inadequacy were manifesting themselves in the form of depression. What were her *real* problems? I eventually helped her to see that the very strong feelings attached to her failure at school, many years before, had been considerably strengthened by the censorious attitude of her perfectionist parents. She had always been made to feel a failure; strong negative emotions were constantly erupting into her conscious mind. In order to compensate for this she had taken on a job that was far beyond her capabilities. Pressure from within and without had become far too much for her, so she had collapsed into a state of almost complete inactivity. She couldn't face life, and her mind had created a state known as a nervous breakdown in order to help her to escape from the intolerable situation. Through counselling, all this was unearthed, faced, and brought to God for His healing power to cleanse the memories of their pain. She eventually changed her job and became a fully released person.

Mr B was totally obsessed about morality and carried his war on pornography to pathological extremes. He was very depressed. On examination I discovered that he had not had intercourse with his wife for fifteen years. Deep down, strong guilt feelings had always been attached to sex from the days of his childhood exploits. When it was all brought to the light, God freed him from it all.

Mrs C was obsessed with cleanliness. She washed herself about twenty times each day and was always quite unnecessarily laundering her clothes. Her life had become impossible and she was continually screaming with anger or collapsing in tears. This problem had brought her marriage virtually to an end. Her *real* problem, of course, had nothing to do with cleanliness. Her case turned out to be one of excessive guilt relating to the secret immoral life she had been living. Once it was exposed, God healed her of it all.

Two cases of "voices" had very different causes. Mr H's voices, which spoke blasphemies whenever he prayed or went to a Christian meeting, were in fact, echoes of his own extremely sensitive conscience. He had been rejected by his parents when he was very small and this led him to be terrified that his blasphemies would also cause God to reject him and send him to hell. Mr Y's voices, however, were of satanic origin. They began at the time when he first engaged in "Ouija", in order to receive messages from dead relatives. Voices certainly came to him—the voices of what the Bible terms familiar spirits, which plagued and tormented him without mercy. Insight into the condition of these two men, followed by intense counselling and divine healing for Mr H and deliverance ministry for Mr Y resulted in both men being completely restored to mental health.

One young woman was frightened of hurting people and especially terrified that she might murder her younger and more vulnerable brother. She did have a problem, but not the one she thought she had! It turned out that she was miserably unhappy at a boarding school and yet, at the same time, she was frightened of her own deep feelings of having failed, or even of being rejected by her parents if she ran away or asked to leave. God healed her through the insight of her parents and a simple change of schools.

I have cited these examples to illustrate the fact that the real causes of mental illness lie deeply beneath the surface manifestations of symptoms and behavioural problems. In this respect we can draw a parallel between physical and emotional sickness. Both our bodies and our minds have built-in ways of indicating that all is not well. In the case of physical illness, a doctor will first listen to a description of the symptoms (the distress signals) as they are being felt by the patient. He will then try to diagnose the *real,* deeper trouble causing them.

The same is true of mental illness. We receive the distress signals in the form of pain in the mind like fear, depression, tension, anxiety or the drive toward compulsive behaviour. These symptoms indicate that hurt or environmental pressures are driving us beyond our ability to cope. It is the mind's built-in defence mechanisms that may take the pain down escape routes into such extremes as loss of memory or even into a fantasy, delusory world of its own creation. Obviously *help is needed and healing must be addressed, not merely to the symptoms but the real, underlying problem.* Thankfully, God, who designed the workings of our mind, is also able to make contact with the innermost core of our being and thereby the real cause of our pain. Further, as we cooperate with Him, He is able to apply the healing balm of His Spirit to the very point of need and truly make us *whole.*

6 COMING FOR GOD'S HELP

A psalmist once described the intimacy of God's knowledge of us in the following words:

O Lord, Thou hast searched me and known me!
Thou knowest when I sit down and when I rise up;
Thou discernest my thoughts from afar.
Thou searchest out my path and my lying down, and art
acquainted with all my ways ... .
Such knowledge is too wonderful for me;
It is high, I cannot attain it ... .
For Thou didst form my inward parts,
Thou didst knit me together in my mother's womb ...
my frame was not hidden from Thee,
when I was being made in secret.
(Ps. 139:1-3, 6, 13, 15)

The Good News which the Bible proclaims, therefore, is that God not only knows our innermost, conscious, subconscious and even unconscious self (see diagram B page 29) but that He is willing and waiting to heal us perfectly. He wants to touch our minds, emotions, and our wills and so make us completely whole. The Bible also indicates that because our heavenly Father did not make us as robots, but instead gave us freedom of will, He awaits our wholehearted response to His offer of healing love:

Behold, I stand at the door and knock; if anyone hears my voice and opens the door, I will come in to him and eat with him, and he with me. (Rev. 3:20)

33

This patient waiting by God for our acceptance of His offer to flood our beings with His presence is beautifully portrayed in Holman Hunt's famous painting, "The Light of the World". There we see Jesus, crowned as the King of kings, humbly holding a lantern in His hand, while gently knocking upon a heavily barred door. This picture depicts the truth that God will never gate-crash the door of the human heart. The handle is only on the inside, and so it is we who must turn it and invite Him in.

In order to avail ourselves of God's help, therefore, we must first believe He exists (Heb. 11:6), then that He is love, and then really open up ourselves to Him at every depth. Divine healing is not mechanical or magical; it is extremely *personal;* it flows from Person-to-person and there must not be any *pretence* about our dealings with God. We must be *absolutely open* with Him. We must expose ourselves to Him by laying bare all our hurts and bruises, all our worries, and all our fears.

It is also important in our approach to God that we do not try to make demands on Him as if we had *merited* His help and healing. We cannot bargain with Him. All He asks is that we simply cast ourselves, without reserve, upon His everlasting mercy and grace. Jesus, in fact, taught the right way in which to approach God in a story about a Pharisee and a tax collector (Luke 18:9-14). Both these men, He said, went at the same time into the same synagogue to meet with the same God. The Pharisee, however, spent all his time reminding God that he was a real success as a religious person, having correctly observed all the known religious observances and having carried out many good deeds. Jesus said that this man in fact never met with God at all because he was blinded by his own self-importance and self-righteousness. By contrast, the tax collector simply exposed his deepest needs by crying out, "God be merciful to me a sinner." In this case, the *real* person truly opened his heart to the being of God, and thus there were positive results.

The fact is that God does not require any of us to attain a certain religious or moral standard before He will meet our needs. He has further shown His mercy, grace and everlasting love for us, just as we are, by giving His only Son to die upon the Cross, in order to deal with all the consequences of our sins.

> *He does not deal with us according to our sins, nor*
> *requite us according to our iniquities.*
> *For as the heavens are high above the earth,*
> *so great is his steadfast love towards those who fear*
> *him; as far as the east is from the west,*
> *so far does he remove our transgressions from us.*
>
> (Ps. 103:10-12)

A hymn writer once beautifully expressed the way in which to come to God in the following words:

> Just as I am, without one plea
> But that Thy blood was shed for me,
> And that Thou bidd'st me come to Thee,
> O Lamb of God, I come!
>
> Just as I am! Thou wilt receive,
> Wilt welcome, pardon, cleanse, relieve,
> Because Thy promise I believe,
> O Lamb of God, I come.
>
> (Charlotte Elliott.)

God has no idealistic, unrealistic picture of us. He knows all about our failures, our regrets and our guilt, but He loves us just the same. There are conditions attached to our receiving His healing power into the depths of our being, but they are concerned with openness and reality, not with moral success

35

and spiritual attainments.

> All the fitness He requireth
> Is to feel your need of Him.
>
> (Charles Wesley)

The testimony of so many sufferers has been:

> I came to Jesus as 1 was,
> Weary and worn and sad,
> I found in Him a resting place
> And He has made me glad.
>
> (Horatius Bonar)

All this means that we can come to our heavenly Father, *confident* that He will receive us. In no way is He going to reject us or turn us away.

Jesus taught us that we must come to God *expectantly.* He said, *"Therefore I tell you, whatever you ask in prayer, believe that you receive it, and you will"* (Mark 11:24). This means that when we have come to God for His healing power to fill us, we must really believe that He is at work within us and also constantly declare this fact to ourselves, to our loved ones and to anyone else who asks us how we are feeling, even while lingering symptoms are still being felt. We should always make confident, expectant statements based on faith and say, "God is healing me." When we make such statements we are expressing our *faith* and not our *feelings.* We are asserting the confidence we have in God and declaring our expectations that He is healing us. Sooner or later our experience will catch up with our statements! This is not just ideas about "the power of positive thinking" or the rule of "mind over matter". We are not merely stating our rather wishful hopes. Our confidence and expectancy have a sure, strong foundation; they are based upon all that God has revealed himself to be as the healer of His children to the depths of their beings. Further, these words assert what we know to be true; that because we have responded to God's love, there must be a sure, happy, positive outcome to our approach to Him. Our attitude can always be that of the psalmist who said constantly to himself, "*hope thou in God: for I shall yet praise him, who is the health of my countenance, and my God*" (Ps. 42:11, King James Version).

Finally, as we contemplate the vastness of God, and realise that He knows what is best for His children, it is obvious that we should come to Him *submissively*. A biblical expression of this attitude is to be found in the picture of God as the Master Potter, with us as the clay being moulded by His hands (Jer. 18:4-6). We can place ourselves, our past, present and future; our hopes and our fears; our desires and our ambitions; our failures and our successes, into His loving hands. We can safely surrender to Him love, absolutely and completely, to an extent, to a depth beyond anything which human lovers would ever dare to do. We can yield to Him and literally abandon ourselves to His loving care. Our inner being is like a house which, over the years, has become dark, dirty and dingy. Now we are flinging open every door and every window, including the attic and cellar, to be invaded by God's light and love. We can feel the breath of His Spirit blowing through us. Isn't it exhilarating? "*Your life is hid with Christ in God*" (Col. 3:3). We can say:

> I surrender all
> I surrender all
> All to Jesus I surrender
> I surrender all.
>
> (W.S. Weeden)

When we place ourselves unreservedly into God's hands in this way, then our healing becomes His responsibility, and He is willing to accept that fact without hesitation or reserve. Once we have responded to His initiative and come to Him openly, realistically, honestly, confidently and submissively, flinging ourselves upon His grace without qualification or reserve, we can be certain that:

"He who began a good work in [us] will bring it to completion ..." (Phil. 1:6).

7 WAYS IN WHICH GOD COMES TO US

God has promised that if we draw near to Him, He will certainly draw near to us (James 4:8). We have seen the manner in which we should approach Him, so now we can study the ways in which we can expect Him to come to us. This presents difficulties because He is Spirit and we cannot literally see, hear, touch or feel Him. Thankfully, however, He knows our frame, He remembers that we are but dust (Ps. 103:14), and therefore He is able to use the gateway of our senses in order to help us apprehend His presence and enter into deep, inner communion with himself.

One of the most familiar ways He has ordained through which He will certainly come to us is through *the laying on of hands* (e.g., Mark 16:18, James 5:14). It has always been my practice in helping hundreds of people suffering deep mental pain to minister God's loving, healing power to them in this New Testament way. The fact that God has indeed reached into their beings through the gateway of the sense of touch has been well attested in scores of testimony letters. One sufferer wrote, "The Lord has healed me after the laying on of hands by you. I am sixteen, and came out for prayer as I was feeling very suicidal and was suffering chronic depression. After ministry I went home on Wednesday night not sure whether my peace of mind would last, but it has! I do thank you sincerely for praying for me, and of course the Lord for healing me."

An older lady delightedly declared, "On the day I came forward to you, the love shone through your eyes, and I knew this was the love of Jesus. From that day I was able to

39

give up drugs and all psychiatric treatment (the psych-iatrist said there was no longer any point in going to see him, I was so much better). The tears and the futility I felt have gone, and there is new life for all of us."

I have usually exercised this ministry in the context of joyous happy worship, with a whole congregation praying for each person as I have laid hands on them. However, the ministry can be used in much quieter services, and many ministers link it very closely with the receiving of the bread and wine in the reverent, beautiful and devotional atmosphere of the Communion service. It can also be used in the quietness of a church vestry, or, of course, in a home. It must be remembered that God doesn't only use ordained ministers of churches as channels of love for the healing of the emotionally sick in this way; the laying on of hands can and *should* be used by those who have been appointed to work in a spiritual-healing relationship with needy people. The important factors are:

- The ministry is an expression of compassion;
- It is lovingly given, and willingly received;
- Both minister and patient are deeply concentrated upon God and open to His healing power;
- There is no fear of interruption, nor undue haste;
- The laying on of hands should always be accompanied by spoken prayer.

When exercised by a minister of the Christian Church, this beautiful ordinance can be accompanied by anointing with oil (James 5:14). Oil is itself an age-old medication and is always associated with a gentle, soothing, healing effect (Luke 10:34). In the Bible, oil is also a symbol of the presence and power of the Holy Spirit of God (e.g., 1 Sam. 16:13). Jesus himself ordained its use in ministering to sick people (Mark 6:13).

A recent book stating a Roman Catholic point of view, *To Heal as Jesus Healed,* * reminds us that early in Church history consecrated oil was used by *all* Christians for "the needs of the members of their household" (p. 19).

In the new Roman Catholic rite the priest prays over the oil:

> Send the Holy Spirit, man's helper and Friend upon this oil which nature has provided to serve the needs of men.
> May Your blessing come upon all who are anointed with this oil, that they may be freed from pain and illness and made well again in body, mind and soul.
> (p. 96)

The testimony of the centuries is that God's Spirit *has* entered into the very depths of believers' hearts as they have sought His gracious influence by being anointed with oil.

I can well remember a dramatic, instantaneous healing of a lady who came to our church having suffered from severe depression for several years. She had been treated in psychiatric hospitals on four occasions but was no better. She was due to be admitted again on the very next day. She told me that every day when she got out of bed she would cry out in agony, "O God, not another day!"

She also had felt totally unable to cope with caring for her four children. Even as I ministered to her, she was sobbing uncontrollably. I began to feel that she was too distressed to be receptive to God. In some desperation I

---

* Barbara Leahy Shlemon, Dennis Linn, SJ and Matthew Linn, SJ (Ave Maria Press).

quickly reached out for the oil that was on the Holy Table behind me and I began to pour it over her forehead. Immediately she became quiet and extremely peaceful. Later she declared that as she felt the oil trickling down her face she knew that she was "soaking up the Holy Spirit as a sponge soaks up water." The next day the psychiatrist was astonished at the change in her and put off her admission into the hospital. In fact she never went into a psychiatric hospital again, but she grew stronger and stronger as the months passed by. Her radiant testimony as to how God came to her through the anointing with oil has brought hope to hundreds. She and her husband themselves now have an effective ministry of healing in the power of the Holy Spirit.

It has become increasingly common for me to see people actually fall to the floor during the ministry of the laying on of hands, as they have been overwhelmed by God's own anointing of their lives. This phenomenon is a feature of the ministry of many people whom God has called to pray over the sick today. With this "resting in the Spirit," one is aware of an experience of being deeply relaxed in a state of both peace and bliss. Despite being definitely conscious of what is happening around oneself and being able also with little effort to rise up from the floor, there is nevertheless a real feeling of resting in the very arms of God and of knowing that He is doing a profound work in the depths of one's being. It is for this reason that people enjoying this working of God in their lives should not be rushed to their feet by well-meaning helpers!

Letters and testimonies I have received have also shown that on such occasions God is definitely at work in a person's life healing memories and applying the balm of His Spirit to emotional shocks or hurts. Burdens are being lifted; chains are falling off; prison doors are being opened, and love, joy and peace are flooding the soul. At that moment people are wide open to all that God wants to do in them; they are indeed like clay in the hands of the potter. Biblical teaching and the experience of countless people confirm that God does visit and heal us in body, mind and spirit through the laying on of hands and anointing with oil! They are part of His prescription for healing!

Another, just as certain, way through which God has promised to come to His suffering children is through His deeply penetrating, all-powerful Word. It was, in fact, a psalmist centuries before the birth of Christ who first saw that God uses both His *spoken* and His written word in the ministry of healing. Of the sick he wrote: "They cried to the Lord in their trouble and He delivered them from their distress. *He sent forth His Word and healed them*" (Ps. 107:17-20).

Two other precious promises concerning the effect of God's Word appear in the Old Testament: "But I, the Lord will speak the Word ... and perform it" (Ezek. 12:25; see also Numbers 23:19) and "So shall my word be that goes forth from my mouth; it shall not return to me empty, but it shall accomplish that which I purpose, and prosper in the thing for which I sent it" (Isa. 55:11).

We are all accustomed to the power of human words. They are the main vehicle we use to express ourselves to one another. Our words have power to bless, help and encourage, or to hurt, wound and destroy. This is true whether the words are spoken in conversation or written in a letter. Our words can go very deep and still be having an effect upon a person many years after they were uttered. People to whom I have ministered have often been suffering from words which were addressed to them long ago by their parents, close relatives, or people they thought to be their friends. Many years after they were actually spoken, such words can still be deeply lodged in their souls, their subconscious, or even their unconscious minds. If human

43

words can have such power for ill, how much more powerful is God's Word for good! God's Word is far more powerful than mere human words can ever be, and His words are always intended for our benefit and for our healing, even if sometimes they do make us feel uncomfortable for a while!

Let us reflect on the amazing things that God has accomplished simply by speaking His Word. In the beginning God actually spoke our universe into existence. "God said, 'Let there be light', and there was light" (Gen. 1:3). Later His Word took on a human form in Jesus (John 1:14). God spoke to us clearly and unmistakably through His Son (Heb. 1:1-2). It is not surprising, therefore, to read that Jesus only had to utter a word of command and a storm was stilled (Mark 4:39). He spoke healing to the sick (e.g., John 5:6-9; Mark 2:9-12; Luke 7:7-10) and even life to the dead (John 11:43, 44). Jesus simply uttered the Word and whatever He willed came to pass. "Jesus Christ is the same yesterday and today and forever" (Heb. 13:8). He has risen from the dead, and He still speaks the same word of healing to the sick today. It is important in healing that we learn to hear and receive that Word, which God speaks directly to our condition. *As we hear, receive, mark, and inwardly digest it, we shall be healed.*

We can expect God to speak to us in church because He has promised to be present whenever two or three are gathered together in His Name (Matt. 18:20). He is present in order to speak to those who are assembled to meet with Him. We must remember that He is not only interested in the crowd as a whole, but in every separate individual person who is present. He knows each of us better than we can ever know ourselves. Jesus stressed the intimacy of God's knowledge of us as individuals when He said: "even the hairs of your head are all numbered" (Matt. 10:30). In the church, His voice may come to us through hymns, the words of the service, the prayers, the Bible readings or the sermon. Through these things He will touch a chord in our hearts.

God, however, is not confined to church services when He wishes to speak to us. He can put His word on human lips in the everyday contacts of life. He may speak to us through the helpful advice or even chance remarks of loved ones, friends or acquaintances. A lady once wrote to me telling me that on a day when she was feeling down, she overheard two people talking on a bus on which she was travelling. What they were saying about someone they knew exactly fitted her own condition and God spoke comfort and help to her through these ladies who didn't even know that she was listening!

The voice of God may also be heard through a doctor or psychiatrist, even when they are unbelievers! We can be sure of this because the Bible itself tells us that God often used people who did not consciously know Him to serve His purposes (2 Kings 5:1; Gen. 50:20; Isa. 45:1).

The most objective, definite and special place where we can hear what God is saying to us is in the words of His own book, the Bible. Esther, whose moving testimony appears in this book (Appendix 1), has become very versatile and practised in hearing and trusting God's written Word, especially as it comes to her through the inspiration of the Holy Spirit. Many more like her have learned the art of searching in the Scriptures and finding pertinent passages, then get lasting benefits from printing them on cards, learning them, and then placing them in key positions in the house (such as over the sink or over the bed) as an ever-present reminder of what God has very definitely said to those who trust Him.

Although God's word may come to us spontaneously through all life's situations and experiences and through all sorts of people, nevertheless *I am convinced that meditation upon Bible stories and upon God's promises in His Word is of vital importance for the healing of the mind.* I have selected some "words from God" and explained how to use them in meditation at the end of this book. Such meditation involves discipline and time in order really to understand at depth the loving and powerful nature of our heavenly Father and the unfailing richness of His promises to those who will lay hold of them by faith.

As we use these words, let us remember that they *are impregnated with the power of God the Holy Spirit himself.* When really digested they release more spiritual healing power into the spirit, soul and mind than tablets can ever do into the body. These words will work for us when we need them and, because they are God's words, *they will perform that which they promise.*

These words will in fact reach the very depths of a person's being. The Bible itself strains at human language when it tries to describe the actual penetrating power of God's Word. It says, *"For the word of God is living and active, sharper than any two-edged sword, piercing to the division of soul and spirit, of joints and marrow"* (Heb. 4:12). As we meditate upon God's Word we can feel it soaking deeper and deeper down into our hearts until it reaches the spirit, the very source of our life and being. It will be doing its work of healing below the level of the consciousness, healing memories, binding together the pieces of a broken heart, and bringing release to those areas which are bruised, long after the Word has initially been absorbed.

God's Word is not only *powerful and penetrating;* it is also *abiding and permanent* in its effects. This is in contrast to the effects of tranquillisers and sedatives, which will always eventually wear off. Let us remember that Jesus said, *"Heaven and earth will pass away, but my words will not pass away"* (Matt. 24:35). "His Word is life, and health and peace," said Charles Wesley.

People suffering from mental pain and anguish must therefore learn to listen for the voice of God. Then, in just the same way as a musician's ear becomes attuned to perfect pitch, so their spiritual ears will rapidly become sensitive to that which is genuinely God's voice. They must learn also how to *absorb* God's powerful and penetrating Word into the very depths of their being, through learning by heart what God has said and by meditating upon these simple yet profound statements, which are sent from heaven itself to heal them. They must learn constantly to express their faith in God's Word as they joyously affirm, "The Word of God is working powerfully in me," remembering that that which God speaks He will perform, so they will surely one day be able to testify, like the psalmist, "God sent His Word and He healed me!"

8 EXPOSURE TO GOD

Right from the beginning of my healing ministry I have had the joy and delight of seeing sudden, dramatic changes for the better in many people who were suffering from severe emotional illness. One of the first women to whom I ever ministered for the healing of intense mental pain was wonderfully and instantaneously healed through the laying on of hands. This lady told a newspaper reporter that she felt sure that her sanity itself had been saved by the sudden intervention of God at one of my healing services.

For most sufferers, however, the. healing of the mind has been a process rather than an event. Their release into peace and joy has usually involved the gradual exposing of their heart, mind, soul and spirit to God, so that His loving power has been able to penetrate ever more deeply into the areas of their needs. This process can be likened to the peeling of an onion whereby light and air reach layer after layer, until the heart itself is laid bare. Also, like the peeling of an onion, this ministry has often been accompanied by tears!

We have seen that, in order to heal the mind, God's Spirit has first to be allowed completely to invade the spirit area of a person's life (page 29). Once this has begun to take place, then the doorway into the soul area has also to be opened as the sufferer allows God's healing Spirit access into the inner chambers of his being (Rev. 3:20). Divine healing of the soul, then, is the result of cooperation between God and man. This frequently includes not only the patient (I use this term for the sake of clarification), but also Christian counsellors, whose task it is to assist the emotionally sick to expose their *real* needs to God.

It has to be understood that when the depths of our souls are exposed to God, it will always be a very painful, even agonising experience for those who have been severely bruised or have become what Jesus called "broken-hearted." Love, patience, gentleness, as well as firmness is needed on the part of the ministers of divine healing as they help such people undergo this major emotional surgery. It is a task that will draw upon all the spiritual resources, experience, gifts and skills of those ministering, who must be prepared to give the patient a great deal of time and *not let go of him until he is established in health.* Few ministries today are more exacting, yet few are more rewarding, for we are co-workers with God in making men and women whole (1 Cor. 3:9)!

Exposure to God not only requires time and effort on the part of counsellors; even more is required of the patients themselves, who must give adequate time to private prayer, asking the Lord to give them the courage, in His Presence, to allow the deepest thoughts and imaginations, sin, guilt, fear, failure, regrets, shocks and hurts to be revealed. From my own counselling of those displaying symptoms of deep mental pain I would give the following advice:

(1) It is essential to find a quiet, light and pleasant room in which there is no fear of being distracted or disturbed for a period of about an hour. The telephone receiver should be taken off the hook!

(2) The seeker and/or the counsellor should be absolutely sure that everything that may be needed is at hand before they enter into the presence of the heavenly Father. Requirements include a Bible, a glass of water, devotional aids, tracts, a notebook and pen, and perhaps a handkerchief

or tissues.

(3) When settled and relaxed, the patient should pray, recalling the presence, love and power of his Lord and asking for His inspiration and help to be entirely honest so that the secrets of his heart may be truly exposed (Ps. 139:23, 24).

(4) As the Lord reveals areas of pain, the sufferer or the counsellor should make detailed notes about what they are and concentrate at depth on only one at a time, continuing the process in subsequent sessions. It is important to be thorough and not to move on to another item until there is a certainty that God has dealt with each specific need.

I have found that the following are the most important issues which need to be faced in every life:

a) *Sin and guilt.* The Holy Spirit should be asked to reveal all that has lain hidden and unfaced in these respects. Patients have to be warned that to ask the Spirit to do this thoroughly will take time and courage. It will hurt to remember such things as barbed words spoken to loved ones. Although shame will be felt as sufferers relive base acts and their terrible thoughts, it is advisable for them to *write down* those things of which they are convicted by the Holy Spirit. *They must also confess them to the Lord, without trying to find any excuse to give to God or to themselves.*

I have warned such 'penitents' not to linger morbidly upon their sins but to let them be drowned by the love of God, remembering His promise that *"If we confess our sins, he is faithful and just, and will forgive our sins and cleanse us from all unrighteousness"* (1 John 1:9). I have insisted that such biblical promises should be repeated over and over again until the inner assurance of God's forgiveness has been grasped and *felt.* Those who truly repent can be assured that God will, as it were, come behind them in the

51

events of their lives and put everything right for those whom they have wronged (Ps. 139:5; Isa. 58:8 and 52:12). In this exercise of truly receiving God's forgiveness, sufferers must also be told to wait upon their heavenly Father until they *know* that they have been healed from the effects of their sins upon their own souls. Then they must be sure to destroy the paper on which their sins were written down. *They are gone!*

> O Love, Thou bottomless abyss,
> My sins are swallowed up in Thee;
> Covered is my unrighteousness
> Nor spot of guilt remains on me
> While Jesus' blood through earth and skies
> Mercy, free, boundless mercy cries.
>
> (Johann Rothe)

Seekers after God's gift of inner peace must also be taught the truths of the atonement — that Jesus Christ took upon himself the guilt and punishment of sins when He died upon the Cross (Isa. 53:3-6; 1 Pet. 2:24) and that He did this, in fact, before they were born. He is the Lamb of God who has taken away all the sins of the world (John 1:29)— including theirs!

I have always felt it important at this time, despite the theological prejudices of many, to point out the wonderful release that can come through making a confession of one's sins to God in the presence of another believer, preferably a priest or minister of the Church. Such action is entirely biblical. James exhorts, "Therefore confess your sins to one another, and pray for one another, that you may be healed" (James 5:16). It is wonderful on such occasions to remember that Jesus has delegated to the Church His own authority to *forgive* sins (John 20:23). The words of a priest, "Go in peace, for the Lord has put far from you all your sins," can bring untold relief to a soul oppressed by sin and guilt. This, in fact, may be the only way some people will ever really be able to grasp the reality of their forgiveness, itself based upon all that Jesus has done to save us.

b) Closely linked in the sufferer's mind to the feeling of guilt is a sense of *failure*. Therefore at one session of exposure to God, I urge people to write down everything in which they feel that they have failed in their lives. I find that many people have been perfectionists and have expected far too much of themselves. I teach them that they must learn to accept themselves as they really are with all their inadequacies, and then, in order to balance their failures, I urge them to write down all the areas in life where they feel, at least in part, they have succeeded. Usually there are more such achievements than they at first thought existed. I urge them to *thank God* for all these triumphs and to remember that, through His unending resources and almighty strength, He will compensate for all their mistakes. This is true because we are *all complete in Him* (Col. 2:10 King James Version).

c) In yet another session needy people should talk about their *physical appearance* with their Lord. I have found, in my experience, that many depressed people do not like their physical form. They have to be taught that God has made us all to look different from each other because our individuality is precious in His sight, remembering that Jesus taught us the importance of a *right self-love* (Matt. 19:19). They should be urged to keep meditating upon this fact until they can truly say, "Thank you Lord, for making me, me."

d) Another important area in the healing of the mind, which often takes several sessions, is the *healing of painful memories*. During these times with the Lord, all the experiences affecting life in the present must truly be relived with Jesus, as by His Spirit He brings them into

53

consciousness! To do this in real depth, the person may need to go back and imagine that once again he is at the beginning of life in his mother's womb. Perhaps even there he was hurt by the actions and reactions of his parents. Fear and tension in the mother can be transmitted to her unborn child. The mother of a woman to whom I once ministered had been expecting her baby during Nazi persecution. Consequently, my "patient" had lived all her life with a terrible apprehension of imminent disaster until she had prayer for the healing of those pre-natal memories of tension derived from her mother. From that time she became much more relaxed.

It must be further explained that the birth process itself can be very traumatic for the child; some people have, in the moment of birth, had to fight for breath with a cord wrapped around their necks; some have had to be delivered forcefully by forceps. It is important for us *all* therefore to bring our actual birth process to God's healing light. Some people will have suffered acute shock by being told that they were born illegitimate or unwanted. Others find the fact that they were adopted a traumatic revelation. It is very therapeutic for all of us to remember that we are not in this world merely because of some human plan, but by the deliberate foreknowledge of God! (Eph. 1:4, 5.) Long before time began we were part of His plan. During counselling about the birth process, I have found it important to ensure that just as the physical umbilical cord of attachment to a mother was once cut in order to give independent life, so too the psychological and spiritual cords that connect people with either, or both, parents have been severed. All of us, *in order to be mentally healthy, must be free of parental dependence or domination.*

As the process of healing of memories proceeds, God has to be asked to remind the seeker of *relevant events in his childhood.* It is at this point that some have to be asked to face the memory of the most painful experience of all: that of rejection. I have taught them to bring the horror of it to God if possible in the presence of someone who does love and accept them. If they have suffered deeply in this way, then they will almost certainly have become obsessive attention-seekers, employing all sorts of devious ways of demanding the love, sympathy, time and devotion of caring people. This will also have made them over-demanding husbands, wives or patients. Even their present sickness may have been unwittingly produced by their unconscious mind in order to obtain any attention through which they can find security, albeit a false one.

People with needs at this depth are usually to be found constantly talking about illness to others, often complaining about supposed sicknesses to husbands or wives, making frequent, unnecessary visits to the doctor or having prolonged telephone conversations with friends, pastors or counsellors. They make sure that when they cry others are present. Such hurt or bruised people also try to make all their friendships on the basis of their need, and frequently get well enough to keep the interest of a counsellor but never completely well enough to do without help. I have shown such people that the only way out of such emotional immaturity is the brutal facing of the fact, that rejection at a sensitive age has given them a desperate insecurity problem, and that it will never be solved by any of these spurious means. Rather, they must learn to bring their deep problems constantly to God and see themselves really being freed by Him from their tragic condition. In prayer they will be able to grasp that God is *setting them free from all regression into psychological childishness, towards the reality of being a mature person!* "Accepted in the beloved", secure in God's love (Eph. 1:6 King James Version). "Jesus breaks every fetter/ And He sets me free." Several

Psalms, such as 23, 34, 91, 93, 103, 121 and 139, portray the security we all have in God's love.

e) I advise other sessions for the exposing of deep needs, hurts, bruises, and broken-heartedness to include an examination of experiences at school, memories of adolescence, adventures with teenagers of the same and opposite sex, failures and successes in love, married life, or the facing of the prospect of being single; relationships with one's children, and home and family life. Success or failure in social life, lack of fulfilment of ambitions, financial problems, and one's spiritual life should also be examined. All these must be faced with God's help. Patients must also examine whether they are being driven by *a deep sense of inferiority;* for instance, a brother or sister was favoured by their parents or succeeded better than themselves. It must be explained that inferiority is sometimes also related to *physical size*, as much as to a sense of failure. It can drive people, albeit unconsciously, to be too talkative, ruthlessly ambitious, unduly critical of others, always to want their own way, to seek to dominate their married partner and children or even to be always the last into meetings in order to be noticed!

f) *Deep feelings of resentment, bitterness and jealousy* must also be faced if people are to be mature and mentally healthy. Therefore patients must be urged to write down all the incidents and people that may have given rise to these emotions and ask God to deal effectively with them (Mark 11:25). We must all ask God to help us *release* others from those emotional and spiritual debts which they have incurred by their wrongs against us. It must be emphasised that it does not matter whether or not we have just cause for our feelings and actions. We must remember that, whatever its cause, resentment hurts us more than it ever hurts the person who caused it! Also, we must always act positively and practically to restore all broken relationships (Mark 11:25, 26). I once heard of a person who was told by a discerning counsellor that she would not be healed until she had written five letters. At first she was angry and indignant, but eventually with God's help she saw this to be right. She realised God required her to write to five people with whom she had had long-broken relationships. She wrote in the spirit of reconciliation and was soon healed of her mental illness.

g) Finally, I ask everyone I counsel to face the *pride* that may be in their heart, which causes them to feel that their employer, church, club or even God himself cannot really get on without them, as though they were indispensable! It is right, good and healthy for us all to feel useful, but when this gets out of hand in the form of pride, then we can be led into various kinds of stress, tension, irritability and excessive activity. We must learn to live lives at a relaxed pace. Many a physical disability, like a coronary thrombosis, would be avoided if people would face the lies they have believed about their own importance, and act upon the insight gained!

It is in ways like this, in private counselling sessions, that I have taught men, women and young people who have exhibited symptoms of excruciating mental pain to work out their own salvation in fear and trembling, reminding them *"God is at work in you, both to will and to work for his good pleasure"* (Phil. 2:13), applying the healing balm of God's love to their deepest needs. The value of a good and sympathetic counsellor to such deeply needy people can hardly be exaggerated. However, for those who are not so blessed as to have such a Christian pastor or friend, let me say that there is no counsellor better than Jesus himself, the Good Samaritan, *who comes to us where we are,* perhaps bleeding and dying in the Jericho road of life; *He* pours the oil and wine of God's love and will maintain His interest in us

57

until we are entirely whole (Luke 10:25-35). It is He who one day will present us sound in body, mind and soul before His Father's throne (Jude 24).

9 FIGHTING FEARS

I mentioned previously that I discovered the truth that "God helps those who help themselves" when I was a young man fighting my own fears, and I am sure that this maxim is true for all who are seeking to live a victorious life. In the Bible, James expresses the same truth another way when he says, "Faith [in God] apart from works [on our part] is dead" (James 2:26, parenthetical statements mine). So, when we really are trusting God to heal us, then we must also begin to live far more positively than we have ever done before.

In particular, we must begin to put our faith into action by fighting our fears, dealing ruthlessly with all our debilitating symptoms. We must learn to keep in step with God, knowing He will pace our healing at a speed exactly right for each one of us. We must make sure on the one hand that our actions do not lag behind His healing work within us and, on the other hand, we must not try to run on ahead of Him. We must not fret if things are not going quickly enough for us, and we must certainly not allow the impatience of others to harass us into moving beyond the point of faith to which God has brought us. In my experience, with God's help the battle against fear can and will be won, "step-by-step" and "little-by-little".

Those suffering from phobias must learn to advance beyond the realm of their feelings, basing all their actions upon the wondrous fact that God is at work in them, both to will and to work His good pleasure (Phil. 2:13). This truth is echoed in the words, "His Word is working mightily in us—no matter what the circumstance, which I feel or see ... . The Word is working mightily in me" (David Ingles).

To be specific, God requires every sufferer's cooperation so that His healing work may bear positive, definite fruit in their lives, as they set out to do those very things their fears previously prevented them from accomplishing. In my own case, this meant I had to fight my agoraphobia by going back to work, setting out on what was for me a terrifying journey. At first I felt panic-stricken, but as I walked I put my faith in God and clutched hold of a little red New Testament, claiming its every promise of peace and joy. In this way I discovered that God's Word, which I had so painstakingly absorbed, truly was at work in my mind and heart. After several successful arrivals at work I realised that the feelings of panic were not as strong, and they eventually disappeared altogether. This achievement gave me a tremendous feeling of satisfaction and a reason for praising God, which would be completely beyond the understanding of those who have never suffered from agoraphobia.

As my progress continued, I was eventually able to embark upon a training course in evangelism at Cliff College in Derbyshire. Neither the principal, the matron, nor students realised that in their midst was a man for whom even staying a night at the college involved a fearful internal struggle. Night after night, I lay there in my room, wracked with terror, wanting desperately to rush home.. However, God was truly healing me, and through my cooperation with Him, the struggle eventually ceased and joy took its place.

As recently as 1975 I had to fight a new battle with fear when I realised that God was calling me to a world-wide ministry and I knew I had a phobia about flying. Once again I meditated upon God's promises of victory and peace in the Bible and set out in trepidation and fear to tackle this impediment in my life. I thank God that on a recent flight I was so much at peace that the stewards had to awaken me when we had reached my destination!

From my own experience I have found that it is important for sufferers not to try to accomplish hitherto impossible or abnormal fears just for the sake of doing so, because this is a way of "putting God to the test" without any definite purpose for doing so. However, in counselling, I have emphasised that they should never let nerves be the reason for "chickening out" of what they would normally have done quite naturally—for example, going for a walk, going to work, attending church or a social club, entertaining friends, going on a holiday, using a lift, flying, or taking a new post.

I have advised them also to *keep a book of victories,* a diary of all their triumphs over their phobias. Continually reading such a book, especially on dark days, has encouraged and strengthened their faith in God's healing work within them. It has given them renewed hope to look forward to even greater victories in the future.

It is good for people who are fighting their fears to remember that bravery and courage are not the absence of fears but the overcoming of them! People without fear may indeed be *fearless,* but they can never be brave!

In fighting their fears, sufferers always need guidance from some trusted person about what is a reasonable fear. For instance, it is a natural and healthy fear of death that makes us careful when we are crossing a road; but it is irrational to be constantly terrified of death when there is no immediate danger of our passing. The natural fear must be accepted, the irrational one relentlessly fought by applying God's promises to help and keep us healthy in that problem area of our soul.

A good counsellor and adviser is not only needed by those who suffer from fears, but also by those who are afflicted with *obsessions*. In my experience those who are in the grip of this particular illness usually find it extremely difficult to distinguish between normal and abnormal behaviour. This may apply to hygiene where, for instance, a certain standard of cleanliness is most healthy, but where obsessive and compulsive behaviour concerned with washing one's body and constantly changing one's clothes can make life absolutely intolerable both for sufferers and their relatives. The same is true of safety precautions, such as locking doors and turning off gas taps. A general rule is that if the actions have the feeling of compulsiveness about them so that they must be repeated, then they are neurotic habits, and must be overcome by fighting them with faith in God. Temptations to "go back and check" must be fought, one by one, in the knowledge that God is taking care of us, and that we are safe in Him. As His work of inner healing goes on, the grip of obsessions will be loosened. *God actually breaks the fetters, but the patient himself must shake them loose and step out of them.* In this way a book of victories will soon carry a wonderful account of things the sufferer now has no need to do!

People afflicted with phobias, obsessions and *depression* must not only fight their symptoms with God's help but also learn how to *educate their emotions* as part of their cooperation with God's work of healing in their lives. The source of these problems lies in the realm of the feelings and it is my experience that emotions can be taught how to behave themselves. I discovered this in the times when I used to lie awake at Cliff College, trembling with fear. In those fear-wracked moments I told myself over and over again that there was absolutely no need to feel like that in those pleasant surroundings, in the midst of such happy, loving people. I asked myself just what there was to give me cause to be depressed or to be *reasonably* afraid. When the obvious answer was nothing, then I reminded myself that I was feeling irrational emotions and I rebuked these stupid feelings in the Name of Jesus, telling them that I would take no notice of them and that they were not now going to spoil my life. To argue and reason with oneself in this way will be an almost non-stop activity for those who are afflicted with emotional illness. The only alternative to such a struggle is to give in to the emotions, a way of constant defeat. So it is best to keep on reminding negative feelings that God is dealing with them, or to treat them like the devil and tell them to get out.

Once again, in this process of educating their emotions, sufferers sometimes need someone besides themselves to help reassure them that their frightening feelings are without real foundation. I can well remember that at the time when I was afraid that I was going insane, I asked a psychiatrist to explain to me the difference between my form of mental pain and real insanity. His answer was simple. He told me that insane people (better termed psychotics) *were not really aware that they were ill* but were convinced that they were in their right minds, even though everyone else was well aware of the fact that they were out of touch with reality. From that time I was able to tell my fear of going insane that it was groundless, and so it soon disappeared.

On another occasion when I was educating myself against my phobia about flying, I spent some time talking to an air hostess who soon convinced me that I was much safer in a plane than when I was driving my car! Of course the feelings of fear when flying persisted for a time and were aroused even at the sight of an aeroplane, but after my talk with the stewardess, I had new ammunition to throw at my fears! People can likewise educate their emotions by dealing with them rationally, and eventually they find that they can come under their control!

People suffering from depression have perhaps the most difficult task of all in educating their emotions, because their very will to get better can itself be sapped. They need a lot of encouragement from those who care for them; in fact, the feeling that they are truly loved and wanted, despite their illness, is a very important factor in their recovery. A person in depression hears his emotions say such things as:

"You are no good; you're just a hopeless and helpless failure";

"You can't get up this morning; you are too tired and too ill even to get dressed";

"Oh, God! Not another day—you cannot face it";

"You have failed God beyond the possibility of recovery";

"You have committed the unforgivable sin";

"The past is too bad to be put right";

"You are a poor wife (or husband, mother or father)";

"You are ugly, unpleasant, and unlovable";

"You cannot do your job, it is too big for you";

or other variations on similar themes, all negative.

These strong thoughts must be resisted. The sufferer must begin to think positively about himself, basing his thoughts upon scriptural truths such as:

Even before He set the sun ablaze, God planned *my* birth and chose me so that I would eventually stand before Him without any blame attaching to me! (see Ephesians 1:4);

There is a place in His plan for His Kingdom that only I can fill;

He actually ordained me for eternal life (Rom. 8:29-30);

His strength is made perfect in my weakness (2 Cor. 12:9);

He works all things together for good for those who love Him (Rom. 8:28);

I have been born again to a living hope. (1 Pet. 1:3);

Because I am in Christ I am a brand new person (2 Cor. 5:17);

Today is the first day of the rest of my life; therefore it is a day of opportunity and a day well worth living.

When in depression, a person must *think of all that is good and beautiful around him* and do something he really likes such as taking a trip or a cycle ride into the countryside. It will help the depressed person enormously to spend time thinking about what he has been able to accomplish in life, however small, and to "Count his blessings, name them one by one and it will surprise him what the Lord has done."

We should start praising God, in and through everything, and move in positive directions by doing such things as seeking to get a job, even a part-time one, and so avoid sitting around, simply dwelling upon negative thoughts. Perhaps the sufferer can become occupied in meaningful tasks, like baby-sitting or visiting elderly people. He can think about the needs of others and set out to pray for them and serve them (Job 42:10, Luke 6:38).

Further advice I have given to depressives is to make sure that every day has a definite framework and keep to it, making efforts to socialise, enjoy the good things of life, and to be friendly and neighbourly!

People who are fighting their fears and educating their emotions must also *learn to laugh with and at themselves.* Emotionally ill people always take themselves far too seriously, because by nature they tend to be very analytical and introspective. A sense of humour is an enormous help in defeating negative emotions. The feelings that are determined to distress people cannot bear to be taken lightly or laughed at! Enjoying good humour, comedies, jokes, and laughing at life is very good mental hygiene. Jesus had a rich sense of humour (e.g., see Matthew 7:3). We can learn to laugh with God, knowing that as we smile the world smiles with us! We all know the relief given by laughing afterwards at what was once an embarrassing moment!

65

Depressives can look forward to the time when they will actually be able to smile at what is now depressing them.

People suffering from *insomnia* also have a fight on their hands because the devil usually convinces them that sleep is vastly more important than it actually is. Every night they feel worried and frightened that they will not go to sleep and it is this fear, together with the effort they make to go to sleep, that actually keeps them awake! Some also become psychologically dependent upon sleep-inducing drugs and are persuaded by the Enemy that they can never again sleep without them. Such people must learn to fight their fears with two truths; the first is that in times of emergency human beings have gone for prolonged periods of time without sleep and have survived! The second is that in the end a person will always get as much sleep as he naturally needs because the mechanism of our body and mind is made that way! So folks who don't sleep at night often fall asleep watching television in the day.

God has actually promised sleep to His children; He has said, "When you lie down, your sleep will be sweet" (Prov. 3:24) and "He gives to his beloved sleep" (Ps. 127:2). Practical ways of cooperating with Him in this respect are:

Not engaging in a lot of mental activity late at night and not eating too much too late!

Not drinking stimulants, such as coffee and tea, before retiring;

Having a time of relaxation before going to bed;

Reading, lovemaking, and, of course, prayer, are good in-bed activities to induce sleep.

Making sure that you are warm, comfortable and have fresh air in the room, perhaps curling up in the relaxed position of an unborn child;

Not consciously trying to go to sleep but just letting one's thoughts wander about on pleasant subjects.

If the sufferer wakes up in the middle of the night, he must avoid lying awake worrying. He should turn on a subdued light, make a warm drink and pick up a book and begin praying or meditating on the goodness of God.

Once again, as God's process of inner healing continues, the patient will find that he is ever more quickly able to go to sleep.

A person regularly taking sedatives should always take medical advice about reducing them or giving them up entirely. A holiday or some other period of less activity is a good time to win the battle over dependence upon such drugs.

A golden rule for all who suffer from emotional illness is: do not go from person to person telling each one that you are ill, distressed, fearful, and so on. Indulging your symptoms in this way will only strengthen the hold they have upon you. If you must cry (and that can be a good form of relief), then cry when you are by yourself.

Sometimes, when needy people have engaged me on the telephone for as long as an hour, I have later discovered that they have phoned several other sympathetic listeners before calling me. These self-indulgent people are seriously impeding their own progress to health. So, it is wise for sufferers to have only one special counsellor to whom they turn in time of need. This person should not be anyone with whom the afflicted person is emotionally involved (such as a husband or wife). However, the counsellor must be wise, sympathetic and understanding, and know when it is best to be firm. Ministers of religion, trained lay counsellors, (Christian) psychotherapists, or previous sufferers from this form of illness are obvious possibilities. Close relatives must be taught to understand the nature of their loved one's illness and be told by the counsellor how they can best help recovery, by, for instance, not chiding the person for being ill and so adding a burden of guilt on to an already crushed soul.

Another second golden rule for those fighting their fears is: avoid attention-seeking behaviour like the plague. Catch yourself when you are seeking sympathy, and deal with the matter ruthlessly! Let your *words* and your *actions* towards yourself, to your emotions, to your friends, to your relatives and to the devil be based upon the truth that *God is healing you and you are being made whole.* Those who resist and fight steadfastly their fears, obsessions, depressions, and indeed all negative thoughts and emotions through their faith in God find that they become truly liberated people (James 4:7).

10 COPING WITH CONFLICTS

When we are fighting fear, we are seeking to overcome one very strong feeling. An emotional conflict, however, is a much more subtle and concealed enemy, which can cause a person to become even more seriously disturbed, devastated and crippled. This condition is one wherein two or more very strong opposing emotions pull a person in different directions at the same time. The result is acute tension and stress, nerves become shattered, tempers frayed and, in extreme cases, the afflicted person becomes violent or else collapses into total inactivity. His morale may become so completely sapped that he has no desire to go on. He may contemplate or even attempt suicide to draw attention to the fact that something is desperately wrong within him.

A typical case is that of D who telephoned us, and was obviously in great distress, crying uncontrollably and threatening to commit suicide. She explained that despite the very strong medication she had been given by her doctor, she had only grown worse. I invited her to meet me in my church vestry and, during the ensuing counselling interview, I discovered that her real trouble was that she was being torn apart by subconscious conflicts, which were causing and perpetuating her intolerable mental condition.

The first strong emotion was attached to a course of training she was pursuing for which she was not really suited and which, deep down, she absolutely hated. One part of her was desperately demanding escape from an intolerable situation. However, she could not consciously admit to this desire to give up the course because she was being pulled in another direction by a second strong emotion, that of *fear—fear* of failure, fear of having no other useful occupation, and fear of strong parental disapproval as well.

As if that were not enough, she was also being tormented by a second issue she had not faced concerning her marriage. This had turned out to be a disaster and one side of her desperately wanted to get out of it. But because she was also a convinced Christian she felt very guilty about these thoughts and about her desire to get divorced. All this was further complicated by the fact that she was *afraid* lest, having left her husband, she would later discover that he had been the right man for her after all!

With all this going on deep down in her subconscious mind it was not surprising she had fallen into a depressed and hysterical condition. When the sources of her trouble were uncovered and consciously recognised, definite action was taken, and she was soon free of her illness.

Conflicts between the strong emotions of desire, guilt and fear are, in fact, very common in our lives. They relate especially to sexual behaviour, marital breakdown, ambitions, examinations, changes of employment, and so on. Religious people, with strong and high ideas about perfection in all things, are particularly prone to states of deep conflict. St Paul described their dilemma in the words, "No matter which way I turn I can't make myself do right. I want to, but I can't. When I want to do good I don't; and when I try not to do wrong, I do it anyway ... there is something else deep within me, in my lower nature, that is at war with my mind ... Oh, what a terrible predicament I'm in!" (Rom. 7:18-25 The Living Bible). He went on to say that the answer lay in realising that a right relationship with God did not depend upon attaining certain standards but in God's gracious acceptance of us as we are, and being led by the Holy Spirit (Rom. 8:1-16)!

A legitimate pride and an unhealthy fear also often oppose each other at various levels of our minds. I once counselled a person who was torn between a proper pride in his intellectual attainments and standard of living and who was, at the same time, terrified that these attributes would mean his being totally rejected by his very "ordinary" family. Another case was where a Jewish woman was fearful that her rightful pride in her ancestry, which she was unwilling to repudiate, would lose her the love of her Gentile fiancé. Both these people had been reduced to mental breakdown because of the enormity of the unfaced feelings attached to their conflicts.

A love-hate relationship is also a well-recognised source of mental breakdown; for example, when a man may feel totally emotionally dependent upon his wife and yet at the same time hate her unwittingly, for making him feel like that. Sometimes the same sort of deep emotions may be aroused in an unhealthy relationship between, say, a son and his mother from whose emotional attachment he has never been able to break free. A man may also respect and admire his boss and yet unconsciously feel guilty about wishing him dead so that he can take his place.

Mental conflicts, then, are always between two or more equally strong but conflicting emotions, and they usually go on below the level of the person's consciousness. Such conflicts arouse high-powered emotional energy, which can explode in temper or even violence at the slightest provocation. Counsellors should always be on the look-out for these hidden conflicts in patients who are experiencing emotions that are out of all proportion to the problem they are dealing with at the time. For instance, a mother may say that the reason she is constantly screaming at and beating her children is because they are exceptionally naughty, but she is, in fact, without realising it, using her children as objects on which to express her own

71

violent feelings, which are really attached to other deep, unfaced conflicts in her life.

Although conflicts sometimes arouse excessive emotional energy resulting in irritability, agitation, sleeplessness, temper and violence, they also have a way of sapping nervous stamina, making the sufferer feel drained, exhausted, tired and listless to a degree totally unrelated to their daily activities. We all feel healthily tired after a period of hard work, but when a person is always tired, beyond any known physical cause, counsellors should search for the energy-sapping conflicts that are preventing the patient from enjoying a really full, healthy and happy life.

Once again, therefore, our study has brought out the need to have a wise, understanding counsellor who will help us to unravel the emotions battling against each other in the depths of our minds, causing us to feel edgy, depressed, moody or even hysterical. Much, however, can be accomplished by each one of us, *ourselves,* once we have understood what the conflicts are, the sorts of emotions involved, and how they can affect our lives. My own personal practice is that whenever I feel something disturbing my peace, I *make* time to be alone with God. I know He doesn't want me to be unhappy, irritable, depressed or difficult to live with. I know He is with me as I open my heart to Him, in order that He may make me whole. I relax and pray, "Search me, O God, and know my heart and reveal to me my secret thoughts" (see Ps. 139:23, 24 and 19:12).

With His help, I ask myself, When did I begin to feel uneasy? What was being said? What was I doing? or What was I thinking about? I want to face my conflicts, my desires, guilt and fears. I know it's going to be a disturbing time with God as my conflicts are exposed, but I know it's going to be worth it in the end! I know that I must, at all costs, be honest with myself.

My notebook and pencil are always in hand because writing things down has a way of clarifying issues and making me face them. Slowly the revelations come! Sometimes I have to cross sentences out as not being really true or honest. I am brutal with myself, knowing I must write down precisely what I *really feel*.

Once this exercise has been completed I ask myself, Is there any *action* I can take that will resolve the crisis? Perhaps I must overcome my fear and really lovingly confront a certain person about the way he has been behaving towards me. Perhaps, despite my fear of being short of money, I must place my trust in God's provision and cut down the number of healing meetings I am taking in order not to feel overwhelmed by my itinerary. Once I have decided this I definitely risk the disapproval of pastors upon whose good opinion I had depended, and refuse to engage in seven-day missions, which they were requiring me to take and yet which I found exhausted me! In such ways I have discovered that action can sometimes, by itself, resolve a conflict.

This also happened when the young lady I have mentioned gave up her course of training, discovering as so often happens that her fears of failure and of parental disapproval had been totally unfounded! The decision was happily accepted by her parents and she made a great success in another sphere of work. Action, then, is often the answer to conflicts.

The deepest emotional crises, however, occur when the sufferer can see *no possible way of escape* from the intolerable situation that has been unearthed. Every suggested solution seems to be impossible for some very definite reason. There is no easy way out of such predicaments for any of us whether we are neurotic or healthy-minded! In this respect I well remember the case of a young woman who told me that her psychiatrist was urging her to engage in illicit sexual activities as a way of solving the conflicts that had built up in her mind. Seemingly, the staff of the hospital where she was being treated even unofficially provided the opportunities for people like her to engage in these so-called "healthy indulgences". What the psychiatrist had overlooked were the deeply Christian convictions that dominated the lady's life. She could never accept the way of escape he had suggested. She finished up in a state of complete confusion and her last state was worse than the first. Eventually she committed her conflict absolutely to God and learned that, although there was nothing she could actually *do* to resolve her conflict, He would, in His time and way, bring her through into quietness of mind. She found peace as she committed every aspect of her problem into His capable hands.

Such absolute trust in God will always bring a *genuine* peace, which is to be clearly differentiated from the spurious counterfeit, which is manufactured by the subconscious mind when the person gives in and collapses into the arms of a doctor or psychiatrist in order to give himself an excuse, for example, to leave an exacting job or for giving up his marriage. Although in this way a respite is gained by the mind having gone down the escape route of a mental breakdown, it carries with it two dangers. The first is that the person will forever feel a "lame duck" who didn't make it. The second is that the mind, once having found this plan of action to give a sort of peace, will continually lead the person back into breakdown as soon as any difficulty arises—so making him into a complete mental invalid. Sometimes this subconscious action can be so drastic that the patient is led into loss of memory or some other loss of contact with reality from whence it is not easy to return. It is far better always to be absolutely realistic, positive and honest about one's conflicts in the first place and face them honestly with God, however terrifying and insoluble they may seem to be.

Once God has revealed the source of conflict to us and we have written them down as honestly as we know how, fully describing the emotions we feel about them, then the enemy has been unmasked and can be overcome. *It is important that we always keep what we have discovered about our conflicts within easy reach of our conscious minds.* We must try not to forget them, nor let the real, inner issues clothe themselves in new disguises and pretend to be something other than they really are.

From the moment the real root of our need has been exposed, its hold upon us will lessen. It will not automatically disappear, but whenever we are feeling alarm, fear or unrest, we will be able to say, "I know what it is that is troubling me, and through faith in God, I am able to cope with it. He will solve this problem as I restfully wait upon *Him.*" The discipline of bringing our spirit, soul and mind to rest in God will prove to be a continual one. We will rarely achieve this soul-rest in a split second. Our conflicts will keep trying to take over, but like St Paul we can and will have the victory over them "through Jesus Christ our Lord!" (1 Cor. 15:57). *We can be sure that God knows us intimately, that He understands the frailty of our human nature and knows better than any of us the predicament we are in. We can rest in the fact that He loves us and will carry us through our conflicts,* making *all things* work together for good to those who love Him (Rom. 8:28).

If you have been trying to cope with conflicts, now, by a conscious and deliberate act, surrender your problems, your hopes, your hurts, your fears, your past, present and future, the whole of your life and being into His hands. And keep on doing this! Picture yourself as resting calmly in two huge, cupped hands, the hands of God. *Keep yourself there!* Keep putting yourself there whenever anxiety, tension, stress or fear arises. Remember then that you are His responsibility. He will lead you, guide you and eventually bring you through into light, joy and peace. In the meantime He will give you grace and strength to cope with the crisis as you live with it until, in His time and way, He will ultimately solve it. He has promised: "God is faithful, and he will not let you be tempted beyond your strength, but with the temptation will also provide the way of escape" (1 Cor. 10:13).

He has never promised life will be easy, but He has promised you that He will give you strength through all life's situations.

The Bible says, "Dear brothers, is your life full of difficulties, and temptations? Then be happy, for when the way is rough, your patience has a chance to grow. So let it grow, and don't try to squirm out of your problems. For when your patience is finally in full bloom, then you will be ready for anything, strong in character, full and complete" (James 1:2-4 The Living Bible).

So let your conflicts drive you ever closer to God. Live with Him in them and through them. I have seen men and women grow into ever greater maturity as they have learned to face their problems honestly with God. I have seen many come into new realms of joy and happiness as a result of coping with crises through faith in Him.

It is only as you love and serve God, *at peace with your own conscience,* that you will be able to live with yourself and finally lie down in rest and quietness, having fought the good fight.

"And the peace of God, which passes all understanding, will keep your hearts and minds in Christ Jesus" (Phil. 4:7).

11 PEACE AMID THE STORM

Emotional conflicts are indeed deeply disturbing, but some of the most terrifying and unpleasant conditions that can assail the mind are better likened to a tremendous storm rather than to an inner battle. Further, whereas conflicts begin unnoticed and usually build up over a fairly long time, these storms or crises can burst upon us very suddenly, when we find ourselves being swamped by mind-shattering circumstances we could never have foretold. We are caught completely off guard as the turmoil breaks out in and around our lives. The emotion engendered by such events is mainly one of *sheer terror and panic. All our securities seem to have been shattered and, as we desperately seek something to cling to, we find that nothing can bear the weight of our distress.* Everything seems to be going down with us! We are seemingly helpless and hopeless, sinking and drowning.

In such crises, life seems very much to be like the storm described by a psalmist in the words, "... the stormy wind, which lifted up the waves of the sea. They mounted up to heaven, they went down to the depths; they reeled and staggered like drunken men, and were at their wits' end. Then they cried to the Lord in their trouble" (Ps. 107:25-28).

We also have a very significant and graphic description of a storm in the New Testament:

"And a great storm of wind arose, and the waves beat into the boat, so that the boat was already filling. But [Jesus] was in the stern, asleep on the cushion; and they awoke him and said to him: 'Teacher, do you not care if we perish?' And he awoke and rebuked the wind, and said to the

77

sea, 'Peace, be still!' And the wind ceased, and there was a great calm. He said to them, 'Why are you afraid? Have you no faith?' And they were filled with awe, and said to one another, 'Who then is this, that even wind and sea obey Him?' " (Mark 4:37-41).

These incidents teach us so much about the storms of life:

- *Their suddenness*—coming with little or no warning;
- *Their force and violence*—the waves beat into the ship so that it was almost full;
- *The natural reaction of fear and panic;*
- *Desperate actions*—as when the disciples desperately searched for help.

The difference between Jesus and the disciples in this terrifying situation was that whereas there was a storm raging in the disciples' hearts, Jesus was able to maintain an authoritative peace which was the outcome of His continued and confident faith in the Father. How wonderful it is when we too can experience a peace like His in the midst of the storms of life.

Since I publicly embarked upon a healing ministry, hundreds of people have phoned, written, attended meetings, or even turned up at my door in states of complete panic because of the storms raging in and around their lives. Their different situations have been, like the waves in the Sea of Galilee, real, and it would have been both dishonest and useless for me or any other counsellor to try to pretend that either the storms didn't exist or that they were less fearsome than the people described.

The elements of the crises in these folk's lives varied considerably. Some people, for example, were in a state of panic because of the threat or advent of serious illness, especially cancer. One can well imagine the extreme alarm of ladies who discover a lump in their breast, or of people who learn that a loved one's illness has been diagnosed as cancer. Other storms have involved:

- *Accidents*—in cars, motorcycles, or the home;
- *Bereavements*—the actual loss of someone nearest and dearest;
- *Domestic problems*—marital breakdowns, teenagers leaving home and so on;
- *Trouble with the police* or impending lawsuits;
- *Situations involving loss of money,* property, reputation or liberty;
- *Satanic attack*—through being cursed, assailed by witchcraft, or persecuted by occultists;
- *Unemployment,* business failure or unfair dismissal;
- *Spiritual breakdown*—the feeling of having deeply offended God, losing His blessing or having blasphemed against the Holy Spirit;
- *Problems involving sex, romance, infatuation,* broken engagements, desertion after being involved in illicit intercourse, rape, unreturned affection or discovery that the person is basically a lesbian or homosexual;
- *Intense mental pressure, worries, anxieties* to the extent the sufferer believes he is going insane, perhaps going to kill someone or even fears that he himself might be murdered.

The list is virtually endless. In some storms it seems that several of these overwhelming events occur or threaten to happen all at once—as Jesus put it, "... the rain fell, and the floods came, and the winds blew and beat upon that house" (Matt. 7:25).

When such storms burst, people tend to run hither and thither, turning to this person then to that one, clutching first at one straw and then at another—with nothing secure to hang on to as the house of their life seems to be collapsing or their lifeboat seems to be sinking. Panic, fear and terror assail the mind.

The Bible, however, not only describes storms, it is full of the testimonies of those who came through such dreadful experiences on to higher ground as they cried to the Lord in their trouble. One man sang:

> God is our refuge and strength, a very present
> help in trouble,
> Therefore we will not fear though the earth
> should change, though the mountains shake
> in the heart of the sea; though its waters roar
> and foam, though the mountains tremble with
> its tumult. (Ps. 46:1-3)

> He reached from on high, he took me, he drew
> me out of many waters,
> He delivered me from my strong enemy.
> (Ps. 18:16, 17)

> The floods have lifted up, O Lord,
> the floods have lifted up their voice; . . .
> The Lord on high is mightier than the noise
> of many waters, yea, than the mighty waves
> of the sea.
> (Ps. 93:3, 4 KJV).

Such peace in storms and triumph in crises come not only through crying, "God, help me!" in moments of despair, but through faith in God's steadfastness, reliability and control over all of life's situations. Psalm after psalm indicates that the writers had *no easy victory* over the harsh, real and terrifying forces assailing their lives. But when it was all over, they were able to thank God for the spiritual lessons they had learned, which would stand them in good stead for the future and also enable them to help, inspire and encourage others who were going through similar crises (2 Cor. 1:4).

I have learned many lessons through the experience of storms in my own life and through listening to the stories of others who, by God's grace, have learned the secret of peace.

One definite secret of success is to remember that the storm raging deep within one's *own* heart and life is the real problem and not, as it seems at first sight, the events happening outside. We see this in the case of Jesus and His disciples. They were going through exactly the same crisis, but their inner state hardly bears comparison! Jesus had such peace that He could actually fall asleep in the storm, while the disciples were in abject terror! In another incident recorded in the Bible, mortal men, like us, portrayed the same inner state of peace in a most desperate situation and appalling conditions in the maximum security wing of the jail at Philippi (Acts 16:24-26). So it is vitally important that the storm in our hearts is the problem to which God's Word must first be addressed, and then we will find that the threatening events around have lost their overwhelming terror.

As we hear God saying, "Peace, be still," to our inner life, we allow this word to soak into our being, convinced that the actual storm around us need not drive us into panic. Action to deal with it must await our gaining an inner peace and confidence through faith in God's providential care over our lives (Phil. 4:19).

St Paul passed through many a stormy situation in his service for Jesus (2 Cor. 11:23-28) and consequently gave some very good advice to fellow travellers on life's rough seas. For instance, He said, "Rejoice in the Lord always; again I will say, Rejoice" (Phil. 4:4) and "in everything by prayer and supplication with thanksgiving let your requests be made known to God. And the peace of God ... will keep your hearts and your minds in Christ Jesus" (Phil. 4:6-7).

Difficult as it may be, we must learn to praise God *in* the storms, praise God *despite* the storms, and praise God *through* the storms. Hundreds of people whom I have met bear witness to the fact that storms do cease at the sound of praise.* This is because praise takes your mind off the crisis and focuses it on God, and the situation is thereby brought into proper perspective.
Further —

- *Praise is a vote of confidence in God;*
- *Praise is faith expressed in words;*
- *Praise puts the devil to flight;*
- *Praise lets off all your pent-up emotions in the right direction, bringing release in the situation;*
- *Praise thanks God in anticipation of victory.*

Let our prayer in the storm be with such words as, "Although this crisis has come upon me, yet I will praise You O Lord. I *know* You are indeed Lord. You have the whole world in Your hands and therefore You have my life in Your hands. I praise You because You are in control. I praise You above this crisis. Hallelujah! You reign. Yours is the power and the glory!"
Also:

- *Praise brings down God's blessing upon our lives.* This is because He inhabits the praises of His people (Ps. 22:3 KJV).
- *Praise bursts open prison doors* (Acts 16:26; Ps. 142: 6-7). We can afford to praise Him with assurance

---

* See books by Merlin Carothers: *Prison to Praise* and *Power* in *Praise* (Logos International).

because He has promised that He will work all things together for good to those who love Him (Rom. 8:28).

A further matter of immense importance for us all is to realise that *the faith we will need in the storms must grow in our times of tranquillity and peace.* People who do not take the necessary time and action to let their faith be rooted and grow in times when all is well will certainly find that it is not there in time of crisis. This is because those who only cry to God in a crisis and do not learn of Him at other times are crying out to One whom they do not really know. To be sure to experience peace in storms, we must spend time in Bible reading, prayer, Christian fellowship, church worship and service when we are in times of peace and blessing so that we build a living relationship with the Lord. Then in times of crisis we will have more than enough experience of the love and power of God on which to base our faith. *No one should wait for a crisis to arise before turning their life to God. Neither should anyone begin to neglect God when their crisis period is over!* If we live close to Him *at all times* we will always be able to sing:

> We have an anchor that *keeps* the soul
> Steadfast and sure while the billows roll;
> Fastened to the Rock which cannot move,
> Grounded firm and deep in the Saviour's love.
>
> (P.J. Owens)

Jesus himself gave sound advice about preparing for storms when He said, "Everyone then who hears these words of mine and does them will be like a wise man who built his house upon the rock; and the rain fell, and the floods came, and the winds blew and beat upon that house, but it did not fall, because it had been founded on the rock" (Matt. 7:24-25). That Rock was Christ (1 Cor. 10:4).

When we have peace in our hearts, we are in the right state of mind and spiritual condition; then with utter confidence, and in the Name of Jesus, we can address the storm outside us. We can speak to it and at it and tell it to be still. At such times we are asserting a spiritual authority that God has promised and actually given to us (Luke 10:19). I often advise people who are going through storms to enlist the aid of other believers to help them to take authority over all the circumstances and situations that are causing panic. The results have been truly wonderful! The storms have abated and there has been a great calm!

In the case of seemingly insoluble problems, all obvious, practical steps must be taken to ease the situation; such action will no longer be based on panic but will be undertaken from a state of quiet peace. God has promised, "In returning and rest you shall be saved; in quietness and in trust shall be your strength" (Isa. 30:15).

With God, and from an inner attitude of peace, broken relationships can now be faced, heartbreaks, rejections and other difficulties coped with, and situations truly clarified without fear; and where necessary, outside counsel, advice and practical help can be sought.

In spiritual situations the storm-assailed person will now be able truly to repent and come to God, firmly assured of His acceptance of him. He will make the necessary confessions and restitutions to people whom he has wronged, if necessary, and seek restoration or admittance to church membership, quietly accepting God's will for his life. Even worries and anxieties will fall into their right perspective as he obediently fulfils God's laws and receives the promised blessings.

My counsel then to all those going through life's storms is to seek an inner condition of calm and then act; look all difficulties full in the face, and work them through with God. By the time the storm has ceased, the sufferers will have learned many deep lessons to fortify them for a more mature, whole and healthy life, secure in God's love.

During the course of my ministry it has been a real privilege to know many who have proved that, with God, it is possible to experience and radiate peace in the most terrible of life's storms. I have seen people come victoriously through the most painful bereavements—for instance in the case of a vicar and his wife who quietly praised God and shook hands with the large congregation at the funeral of their son who had been tragically killed in a motorcycle accident.

I remember also the serene confidence in God of a young wife who had had both breasts removed and was dreadfully stricken with cancer, and the remarkable peace of her husband after her passing. Likewise I recall the joyous confidence of a woman in the face of multiple sclerosis, her situation being made all the more terrible by the fact that her husband had left her on account of her illness.

Similarly I saw the undaunted faith of a man whose business had failed, whose first marriage had broken down, his second wife having left him through no fault of his own, and whose daughter caused him great anxiety by her wayward behaviour; added to that, his church rejected him because of the court cases and imprisonment awaiting him. In the midst of all this God gave him inner peace as he lived in the power Jesus has promised to give all His disciples. From this attitude of peace he quietly took all the practical steps to remake his life. I have seen him win through to a great calm and wonderful happiness.

Nowhere has God promised us an easy life. Storms will assail us all at some time (Isa. 30:20-21, Ps. 119:67, 71); Jesus himself said so! The word 'peace' in the Bible does not mean simply 'tranquillity' or 'the absence of strife' as some imagine. It is better translated 'victory through conflict' or 'peace amidst a storm' (see John 16:33).

We must not be taken by surprise therefore when life's storms burst upon us. We must not feel that God has forsaken us, leaving us entirely in the hands of the devil. When Jesus was among men and women, there was never a circumstance or situation outside His control. The same is true today. He is able to work *all things* together for good for those who love and trust Him. The Bible's promise is true! "Thou dost keep him in perfect peace, whose mind is stayed on thee; because he trusts in thee" (Isa. 26:3).

Every one of us, no matter what our troubles, can know *peace amid the storm,* and see the swirling ocean, which seems about to swamp our little boat, become a great calm!

12 VICTORY OVER EVIL POWERS ·

More than ten years of extensive experience in the realm of divine healing has led me to the inescapable conclusion that some severe emotional disturbances are definitely caused by evil spiritual powers. This is certainly substantiated by the teaching of the Bible (e.g., Mark 5:1-15). It is true that not many psychiatrists or doctors agree with the New Testament teaching that the world in which we live is populated by evil spirits that can oppress or even possess human beings. This is not surprising, because *spiritual truths are only spiritually discerned.* As St Paul said, the "natural" man cannot visualise or understand spiritual realities; they are nonsense to him (1 Cor. 2:14).*

I have, however, personally seen hundreds of emotionally afflicted people healed through deliverance ministry.

T was a rough, non-churchgoing, no-nonsense cockney who came to my vicarage door in a state of terror and shock. A few days previously he had been *dabbling with Ouija* (an occult "game" in which people try to receive messages from the dead by using an indicator, such as an upturned glass and letters of the alphabet). From that moment voices had tormented his mind and unseen forces had taken hold of his massive arms and hands, trying to control them and make him kill his wife. He was becoming more and more frantic and emotionally disturbed. All this immediately subsided when I exorcised the spirits in the Name of Jesus in T's own home.

By contrast, J was a sweet, middle-aged woman, seeking after spiritual truth and reality. Sadly, she sought this in a Spiritualist church, where she took part in seances.

* See my book, *Supernatural Superpowers*

Very soon she began to see hideous faces and other visions, which tormented her even when she was asleep. She told me she was slowly being driven crazy. Once again her troubles ceased immediately after she had been exorcised.

I have ministered deliverance (or exorcism) to scores of people who have become tormented through such involvement in the occult. God has in fact warned us against any participation in occult activities, because they can have devastating effects on our minds and lives (e.g., Deut. 18:10-12).

I have also had to minister deliverance to people who have been solemnly cursed. Among them, I well remember P, a tall bachelor from the Midlands of England; J, a pretty teenaged Chinese girl in Singapore; and M, a bouncingly beautiful West Indian woman. The cursing had in each case resulted in their being almost tormented to death by evil spirits. P's mental condition was accompanied by terrible physical tremors, jerks, twitches and vomiting. J was visited at hourly intervals by a "night rider" who threatened to destroy her in the night and by evil spirits that sent her into unpredictable and unexplainable trances by day. M became excessively violent and destructive and even tried to strangle her only little girl.

Some "possession" cases have resulted in abnormal sexual behaviour. K became gripped in a lesbian relationship through an over-emotional involvement with a middle-aged woman friend. It all began with a little kiss or two, but soon she became ensnared and imprisoned by the devil. F, an Anglican curate, had given way to his sexual feelings for young boys and had consequently become a seemingly incurable homosexual. L had almost jokingly engaged in a little transvestite behaviour and to his horror had discovered that he couldn't break out of behaving like a woman. All were delivered in the Name of Jesus.

Such instances show that indulgence in sexual perversions can undoubtedly lead to complete domination by an unclean spirit. The progression is always the same: first there is the temptation, which is followed by occasional indulgence, then by deliberate, wilful action. During these early stages the person still feels to be in control of the situation. Eventually, a demon moves in through the opened door and the activity becomes completely out of the person's own control. He has become demonised, or ruled by an evil spirit. Sex demons are running rampant today. So too are "religious" demons, which, through a person's indulgence in false religious thoughts and activities, often produce religious mania in sufferers.

Addictions, too, are often the result of demonic activity. Such was the case with V, who sought my help to free her from drug addiction. She had, in fact, become a drug addict after she had tried a "trip" or two, simply out of curiosity. On the other hand, B became an alcoholic as she sought to satisfy her inner loneliness with drink rather than by seeking God's gift of consolation. Such instances, supported by biblical teaching, have led me to see that personal, invisible, *powerful agents of the devil are creating havoc in many thousands of lives* in the non-Christian, curious, undisciplined, immoral and permissive society in which we live.

This assertion is *not irrational.* Once we have seen that a human being has a spirit and soul, and that what affects one of these areas will also affect the others, then the way in which the ministry of deliverance works becomes clear. Let's take another look at our diagram. (See Page 29.)

When people engage in occultism, other forbidden religious activities, or constant, wilful sin, they are opening themselves to the influence, or even entry, of a demonic entity into the spirit area of their being. From this viewpoint the evil entry can influence the whole of their being (mind, will and emotions), even having a devastating effect upon the body. What the Bible terms demon possession is the ultimate condition in which *the whole* of the sufferer's life is controlled by evil spiritual forces.

In the gospel stories it is recorded that these agents of the devil reacted to the holy, powerful presence of Jesus and used the person's mind, lips and body through which to manifest their fear of being cast out (Mark 5:9-13). The same phenomena occurred later, when demons were confronted by Spirit-anointed Christians such as Philip the evangelist (Acts 8:7; 16:18). The same is true in the moving of God's Spirit throughout the world today. I always have to be prepared for such manifestations when I am ministering in the power of the Holy Spirit. The fifteen hundred people present at a meeting I was leading in the Birmingham Town Hall will never forget the moment when, as soon as I rose to my feet, demons began to cry out in that large auditorium and many people had to receive immediate deliverance.

In order for an effective deliverance to take place, the spiritual process by which the sufferer actually became possessed must be reversed. This inevitably involves:

1) *Repentance* of the sin, which opened the sufferer's being to the evil spirit in the first place.
2) *Renunciation* of the devil and all his works by a constant act of will. This may involve the burning of books, destruction of objects, charms, tarot cards, etc., and the total breaking off of all relationships that the devil has used as a means of entry into the person's life.
3) *Turning to Christ* with the whole being and reorientating the life of the spirit entirely towards God.
4) *Living a life of obedience* to God, in accordance with the laws and conditions set down in His Word, the Bible.

5) *Seeking to be filled with the Holy Spirit* so that there will be nothing but God and His goodness filling the human spirit and no vacuum through which the devil can re-enter and repossess his victim (Matt. 12:43-45).

When these conditions have been fulfilled by the afflicted person, the mature, experienced and fearless Christians ministering deliverance should solemnly *bind* the evil spirit so that it can do no further harm to anyone. They should then *take authority over it* in the Name of Jesus and solemnly *cast it* (or them) into the pit to await the judgement of Christ (2 Pet. 2:4). The spiritual umbilical cord with past generations should then be solemnly broken, and the afflicted person's spirit should confidently be *sealed* with the Spirit of God (Eph. 1:13). A great deal of after-care will be needed during the convalescent period; the inner hurts and the emotional and environmental problems caused by the evil spirit must be faced and dealt with in loving care, so that the healing can be complete. Ideally, the delivered person needs to become a committed member of a warm, loving Christian fellowship.

Finally, the afflicted person must be shown the glory and majesty of *Jesus* and the completeness of His victory over all evil forces, so that he can put his confidence in Him for his future spiritual safety. He must be shown how to put on the whole armour of God (Eph. 6:10-18) in order to resist any satanic counter-attack.

If all these biblical conditions have been fulfilled, then deliverance ministry need never be prolonged, abortive, nor frequently repeated. Indeed, for the sake of the patient, it should be as quick and final as the New Testament clearly portrays. If it is not proving to be so, then something is wrong, and there should be disengagement until the source of the impediment to deliverance has been uncovered and removed.

In my experience, the following people may well need deliverance as part of the inner healing process:
• People who have been involved in occultism in any of its forms—spiritism, Ouija, tarot cards, fortune telling, astrology, oriental arts (like Yoga), levitation, transcendental meditation, cults, false religions, mediumism, etc.;
• Those who have, at some time, been hypnotised, thus surrendering their soul to the will of someone else;
• Sufferers from drug, alcohol, or nicotine addiction, or obsessive eating;
• Compulsive thieves, gamblers or liars;
• Those who have reasons to believe that they or their family have been cursed;
• People who feel themselves to be controlled by forces other than God;
• When the onset of the symptoms coincided with involvement in occultism or wilful sin;
• When the patient has kept "bad company" or has been in deep fellowship with those who dwell in darkness;
• People who have been under the very strong influence or domination of another person; this may even have been sexual, or a dependent relationship.

It must be noted that these factors do not automatically indicate the need for deliverance. Exorcism should only be ministered when such people are obviously unhappy, distressed, emotionally disturbed or spiritually ill at ease.

The diagnosis of the need for deliverance should not be allowed to unduly shock or alarm people and they should never be allowed to think that they themselves are "of the devil." Patients must be taught to avoid occult exorcists at all costs, and must be advised not to seek deliverance from Christians who appear to be obsessed with demons or who treat every emotional disturbance or mental illness as a demonic condition. Only mature, Spirit-filled Christians, whose own lives show evidence of discipline and the power of God, should be allowed to deal at such depth with people's lives.

Many of the people who have come to me thinking that they may be oppressed by evil spirits have not in fact been so. *Some have even subconsciously fastened on to the idea that they are possessed in order to avoid the pain of facing and dealing with their real problems!*

However, for those who really have been in need of deliverance, I have always found deliverance ministry to be real, simple, quick and effective. Through such ministry, now practised all over the world, thousands of sufferers have begun to experience the glorious liberty of the children of God (1 John 5:18; John 8:36). For *he whom the Son sets free is free indeed.* Deliverance from evil spirits and subsequent confidence in continual spiritual victory over them, through Jesus Christ, is a most positive and glorious step to maturity and wholeness, peace, joy and happiness.

13 SEXUAL SANITY

It was the pioneer psychiatrist Sigmund Freud who first drew attention to the importance of the sex instinct in mental health. His research convinced him that stresses related to sex were in fact the cause of most mental illnesses. Most psychiatrists today would say that Freud overstated his case, but no one seeking to help disturbed people can afford to discount emotions surrounding sex as a strong contributory factor to mental disease. Certainly, I have at times been almost overwhelmed by the number of people seeking help about problems directly or indirectly related to sex.

Without doubt, strong emotions are aroused by the sex drive, and all sorts of feelings relate to it. Chief among these are guilt, fear, frustration, inadequacy, dependence, disgust, revulsion, anxiety, stress, rejection, shock and sorrow. Non-Christians often blame strong religious taboos attached to sexual activity for the fact that many people never feel free to release their sex urge in a healthy way. This may have been true to some extent in the past, but it must also be pointed out that in the permissive society in which we live, the number of people with problems related to sex seems to have increased rather than diminished.

Christian ministers are often being asked to pick up and try to rebuild the wreckages of lives, smashed to pieces in a society where sexual activity has gone off its God-given rails of disciplines which once gave it safety and direction. The experience of many prove that sex is a beautiful servant, *but when unrestrained it gains the upper hand and can become a terribly cruel and destructive master.*

The change in attitude towards morality in this generation has, in itself, produced *insecurity* on a massive scale. The signposts which used to indicate the difference between right and wrong and gave a sense of direction, have all been removed. This has mainly been at the instigation of commercial interests working through the mass media. The result has been that people today hardly know which way to turn for sound counsel and advice. Consequently, many have become frightened or even panic-stricken and have rushed down the paths of contemporary permissiveness, leading them only further into the labyrinth of chaos. Utterly confused, they break down completely. Frequently faced with this situation, I have given the following advice to those who have sought help:

1) *Accept and come to terms with the fact that the sex drive is a very powerful force in your life.*

If a person doesn't do this, then he is heading for real trouble. By refusing to admit that these feelings are there, he will, in fact, only succeed in pushing them down into his subconscious mind, from where they will surface wearing "other clothes" in order to deceive him. Frequently, these unfaced sexual urges appear in the form of a sinister sense of anxiety, tension or even sheer fear. The deceived person may well find himself being excessively judgemental about other people's failures, obsessively shocked at the behaviour of the society in which he lives, completely unable to form deep relationships himself, be unhappy in marriage, feel deeply guilty about sexual thoughts and acts, and lapse into deep depression. It is extremely important, therefore, for us all to take time to take the lid off our sex drive. Christians who are shocked at such an idea are the ones who need most to follow this advice!

They need to examine their sex drive, face it, even to the acknowledging of the sorts of people, or particular persons, who attract them. As they do this, they need to remember that sex in itself is good, clean and healthy, one of God's most beautiful and wonderful gifts to His children. He made all of us to be sexually motivated people—*and saw that it was good!*

2) Once a person has truly acknowledged the reality and force of his sex instinct, then he must face that which is immature in his personality. Quite apart from the teaching of the New Testament, history itself has proved that the most mature of people are those for whom sexual activity has been the expression of a deep and abiding relationship of commitment to one member of the opposite sex, within the framework of marriage. To seek sexual fulfilment outside of such a relationship usually only brings about frustration, guilt and other personality problems.

We should always remember that a great lover is not a man who can bring fulfilment to several women, but one who can completely fulfil, and be fulfilled by, one woman all the days of his life. The same applies to great women lovers in their relationship with a man. Anything which falls short of this, like masturbation, lust, promiscuity, sexual attachment to a parent, complete emotional dependence upon another, and so on, is a sign of instability and inadequacy. If it is of actual or imaginative genital involvement, then from a Christian point of view it is sinful (Matt. 5:28; James 1:14-15).

The fact that such things are displeasing to God will make a person want to avoid acknowledging that they are there, but if he refuses to acknowledge them he will only get his emotions in a tormented state. We must face our sexual shortcomings and bring them to God for His help in order to overcome them. He knows what we are made of (Ps. 103:14) and has promised to help us to be *total,* man or woman.

3) I counsel people to *learn to face their sexual abnormalities boldly.*

The permissiveness of today's society has brought to light the massive numbers of people who suffer from sexual abnormalities such as homosexuality, lesbianism and transvestitism. What is "normal" sexuality should be apparent to all. It is made plain by the fact that male and female genital organs complement each other and by the fact that the procreation of children is obviously the ultimate goal of our sex drive.

From my experience of counselling emotionally sick people I would affirm that the contemporary acceptance of sexual abnormalities is not at all helpful to those who have them. In order to water down guilt aspects, permissive society invites homosexuals and like persons to accept themselves as *abnormally normal,* a contradiction which can only lead to deeper stress.

It is true that most people go through phases of sexual abnormality and that many retain bisexual tendencies in their lives. For their mental health's sake such people should acknowledge to themselves that their abnormality exists and keep it in their conscious minds where it can properly be dealt with by prayer, counselling and, if necessary, deliverance ministry.

4) Everyone must *learn to face the different sexual phases through which they will pass in their lifetime.*

It is difficult to be absolutely dogmatic about just how these will specifically affect every individual, but a general picture can be portrayed. Freud proved without doubt that when we are young we gravitate towards the parent of the opposite sex (this may in fact be a substitute father or mother figure). He showed that these vague but definite sexual feelings can sometimes be accompanied by guilt, jealousy or hate for the parent who is competing with us for our "beloved's" affection. Most people grow out of this in adolescence, but if the transition is not successfully negotiated it can cause breakdown later in life, through over-dependence upon a dominant mother or father.

Early adolescence is a period when our sexual instinct generally latches on to adults, such as teachers, ministers, movie and TV stars, etc., and also even on to people of the *same* sex. "Fancies" or "crushes" for persons of the opposite sex about our own age can reach great heights and then die just as rapidly. The person once craved after can soon just as strongly be disliked, and that is why marriages contracted in adolescence so often quickly end in failure. Later, as our personality matures, definite sexual orientation towards one desired person eventually becomes established, often resulting in marriage, but if the love is not returned a terrible emotional storm ensues and has to be weathered.

Emotional problems resulting from the sex instinct do not necessarily cease with marriage, for we tend to behave as if we were polygamous animals by nature, even though God created us as spiritual beings and intended us to be monogamous (Gen. 2:24; Matt. 19:6) and our society encourages promiscuity. So our sexual desires can again begin to wander. Adultery or other unfaithfulness is a constant, real temptation to many, which needs a level head, discipline and spiritual maturity in order to resist it.

The change-of-life in the forty to fifty age group also produces all sorts of emotional variations. Married women often have a great urge to be courted and fall in love again. Both men and women want to prove to themselves that they are still attractive to members of the opposite sex and are tempted to have affairs. Both can have a subconscious fear that their sexual powers may be waning and want them to be sparked into flame again.

All this indicates that efforts have to be made to keep sexual activity alive in marriages. It must always be fresh and inspired. Frank discussion between the partners is most necessary and healthy.

Sexual feeling continues to ebb and flow throughout the whole of life, with the general effect being towards a gradual decline in sexual feelings and powers. This varies greatly from person to person.

Even in this brief study we have seen how Freud came to emphasise the place of the sexual drive in relation to mental health to such a great extent. However, millions of happy, mature, stable lives bear witness to the fact that it is possible to enjoy all the pleasures of sex and negotiate all its difficulties through the whole of life by being *honest with God* and with each other, seeking His help to keep this important drive always flowing in good, healthy channels.

5) It is most important to *keep sexual failures in a proper perspective.*

This is necessary because strong religious attitudes have always been attached to sexual licence, resulting in its being regarded as the worst possible form of sin. Consequently, *the guilt which arises out of sexual immorality is out of all proportion to its importance.* The Bible itself is absolutely frank and open about sexual failure, even on the part of some of its greatest saints (e.g., David and Bathsheba, 2 Sam. 11). The gospels show that Jesus, while not condoning sexual sin, was nevertheless always understanding and forgiving towards those who had failed in this realm (John 4:7-26, John 8:3-10), and He had among His closest companions Mary Magdalene, a woman who had almost certainly been a prostitute and had made a total mess of her life.

In today's world, sex appeal is used in many advertise-ments. Sexual activity is frankly portrayed in films, on TV and is highlighted in many magazines and newspapers, and so we are being bombarded from every quarter with what all too frequently are immature concepts of sexual behaviour.

It therefore becomes increasingly difficult to maintain outright sexual maturity, keep sex in its proper relation to the rest of our lives, and avoid sexual failures. Mature sexual failure can occur, and is occurring still in millions of lives. To those, however, who have failed, Jesus still says, "Neither do I condemn you; go, and do not sin again" (John 8:11) and He will give His strength to those who are seeking to find victory and sexual maturity (Phil. 4:13).

6) Finally, we must *learn to discipline and redirect our unfulfilled sexual longings.*

Many people, for one reason or another, have to go through life unmarried. Others lose their partner, whom they feel to be irreplaceable. Few people, if any, can go through life having had all their sexual longings and aspirations fulfilled; consequently, for many people, these unsatisfied longings manifest themselves in sexual fantasies, in erotic day and night dreams, or feelings of emotional stress and strain. Today, in an attempt to meet these needs, more and more people indulge themselves in "soft" or "hard" pornographic books, magazines, films, and jokes. These activities, however, are counterproductive, for the more the "animal" is fed in that way, the bigger and more hungry it becomes.

A much more healthy way out of this difficulty, as we have seen, is to face the power of our sex drive, honestly unclothe it, take off all its disguises, and learn how to recognise it and deal with it, by bringing it openly to God for His help to control and discipline it at all times. With God's help we will not give in to sex's every whim and fancy. We will learn to recognise infantile, adolescent immaturities and gross abnormalities and constantly direct our sex drive along its right and God-given channels. *We will gently but firmly bring every thought into captivity to Christ, under His rule and sovereignty* (2 Cor. 10:5).

This God-given ability to discipline our emotions is a

101

hallmark of spiritual maturity and dependability and it will stand us in good stead for the whole of our lives, in all its aspects.

Such discipline is not the damming up of the stream of sexual emotion so that it builds up intense pressure resulting in emotional breakdown and a rush of uncontrollable behaviour. It means that the torrent of our sexual energies will be *redirected* down chosen channels that are good, beautiful, lovely, fulfilling and of good report (Phil. 4:8). These healthy channels can be art, sport, music, business, community service, home-making, gardening; the options are endless. Above all, these drives can be channelled into the God-given ways of Christian love, devotion, worship, and of dedicated service to God; that is towards the chief end of man, which is to "glorify God and serve Him for ever"! In this way, those often frightening, seemingly uncontrollable, devastating and destructive emotions released by our sexual drive can find beautiful and glorious ends; for some, in a mature, God-ordained, life-long sexual relationship within the fulfilling framework of marriage, but also for everyone in the ultimately only *totally* fulfilling goal life has, that of *a deeper relationship with God, in whom is total health, joy and happiness.*

14   MECHANISMS OF THE MIND

Doctors today take it for granted that the vast majority of their patients have at least a rudimentary knowledge of how their bodies function and therefore know how to keep themselves as physically healthy as possible. *However, comparatively few people are aware of the way their minds work and so lack the knowledge of how to keep themselves mentally healthy.* This ignorance also accounts for much of the misunderstanding that many sufferers from emotional illness have to endure. Even friends and relatives who want to help their "emotionally afflicted" loved ones usually haven't any real knowledge about how, or where, to begin. So, for instance, out of sheer frustration, they are driven impatiently to urge a person suffering from depression simply to "pull himself together", which makes the sufferer feel even more inadequate and guilty and is likely to send him into an even deeper state of depression.

Many of the people I have counselled would never have sunk into such deep states of emotional illness had they and those who were near to them been alert to the mechanism of the mind. It is important to realise that the adage "prevention is better than cure" is just as true for health of mind as it is for the well-being of the body.

Everyone should know, for instance, that the mind has certain built-in defence mechanisms against any unbearable pains that assail it by *immediately pushing them down below the level of consciousness* to a place where they can no longer be felt. (See Diagram B, page 29.)

This is done by the person subconsciously trying to forget, and thereby get rid of, intensely disturbing emotions like shock, fear, guilt, rejection, sorrow, anxiety, insecurity, resentment or bitterness. The mental agony of crises or conflicts may also be deliberately buried beneath the conscious level of the mind. It is important to realise, however, that this natural attempt to obtain short-term relief by refusing to face emotional pain always inevitably brings on long-term problems. This is because although the painful feelings are buried, *they are far from dead.* They live on, deep in the subconscious mind, where they create havoc with the person's subsequent attempts to live a normal life.

An important rule in mental hygiene is to resist the temptation to push painful experiences out of sight and learn how to deal with them in the area of the *conscious* mind as they happen, whatever the cost may be in tears, toil, sweat, fear or sorrow. We must face our traumas head on! It is helpful therefore to *write the problems down, take them to God and bathe them in prayer* until they are truly dead. We should take the advice of the song:

> All your anxiety, all your care
> Bring to (God's) mercy seat
> *Leave it there*
> Never a burden He cannot bear
> Never a friend like Jesus.
>
> (Source unknown)

We know that *God can and will give us a true and lasting peace.*

Another important matter in mental health is that *we should learn to differentiate between what are symptoms of emotional ill-health and what are its real causes.* We should, for instance, never treat depressions, phobias, addictions, obsessions, and the like, as if they were themselves the cause of our troubles. We must realise they are, in fact, *symptoms* of deeper, underlying problems connected with experiences that are so painful that we do not now wish to remember them. In order to be truly mentally well, we must, with God's help, try to unearth the *real* causes of our illness, stripping them of the clothes in which they are at present masquerading so that they can truly be exposed to God's healing love. We are the more likely to succeed if we do this at the first sign of mental disease or disorder; otherwise, the inner deceit will grow and become harder to face.

We should take time to seek out that which is really troubling us, asking such questions as: What is the real reason why I feel so fearful, tense, uneasy or depressed? Why do I want to behave in this irrational way? We must not be content until we have gone past the immediate, obvious answers and reached the deep underlying cause. Further, in our attempts to understand ourselves we must *watch out for all the deceptive tricks our minds will attempt to play on us.*

One such device it frequently uses is that of *projection.* This occurs when a person, without realising what he is doing, projects on other people, or the world outside, what is really in fact going on in himself. We can see how this happens from a simple, everyday illustration. I was once asked to show transparencies of one of my holidays for folk at church. I was amazed to discover that when I showed the first picture, it had a huge black mark across it. I apologised to the viewers, but when the next nine pictures all showed the same fault, I decided to investigate further. The screen was perfect, so too were all the exposures. In the end, I discovered that the lens *inside* the projector itself had a huge crack across it. This was why no matter where the projector was pointed every picture appeared to be blemished. What was needed was a new lens!

It is easy to see how this applies to mental mechanisms. If, for instance, the "lens" of a person's mind is stained with unfaced, impure ideas about sex, then he will inevitably see moral filth and dirt everywhere, even in the most beautiful of relationships. Similarly if he has deep, unfaced insecurities, he will always project these on to the world outside, and see it as hostile, threatening and unfriendly. It is extremely important therefore that we keep our inner being clear of all that would mar our ability to see things as they really are, and not allow them to be coloured by our own presuppositions, warped ideas or insecurities (Titus 1:15; Prov. 23:7).

Very similar to the mechanism of projection is the mind's technique of *transference*. This is the process by which we transfer on to some other person or situation feelings that they do not really merit. An obvious illustration of transference is when a young woman transferred to the man she has married her ideal of the perfect husband. This ideal man however, doesn't really exist, but subconsciously the woman is afraid of acknowledging this to be true because she is insecure and derives a great deal of comfort from her delusion. Both she and her husband are in for a difficult time of tension and stress until the transference has been uncovered and the real security needs in the woman's life have been truly faced. I have known people who have *transferred all their insecurities and hates* on to some other, innocent human being, and by doing so, robbed themselves of healing.

In the same catalogue of the mechanisms of the mind we must place *fixations*. These occur when childhood attitudes of love and dependence upon a mother or father figure have not been jettisoned and have become fixed on to some other person, much later in the sufferer's life. The result can be devastating for mental health, especially when the person upon whom the fixation rested dies, leaving the insecure sufferer with no prop upon whom to lean to derive the necessary support for his immature attitude of dependence.

In order to be mentally healthy we must watch out for any tendency we may have to cling to people for emotional support. It is far better to face up to our need and find our security solely and ultimately in God himself (Ps. 118:8).

We should also be on our guard against two other techniques our subconscious minds may use to try to avoid real issues.

1) *Regression.* This is a resorting to childhood behaviour in order to avoid adult and mature respons-ibilities. When we do this we tend to fall back on methods by which we got our own way or escaped punishment as children. This is a mechanism of the mind likely to affect those who were spoiled or indulged by their parents. Hysterical outbursts of temper, refusal to talk, uncon-trollable crying, self-pity and running away are all characteristic of infantile ways of avoiding real issues that will, in the end, still have to be maturely faced if we are to become whole people.

2) *Rationalisation.* By employing this technique we try to persuade ourselves that our feelings and behaviour are totally reasonable, when actually they are not. We have in fact reached our conclusions on the basis of our emotional needs rather than on rational grounds. One man I counselled had given himself what seemed to him very good reasons for leaving his job, when the real truth was that he was afraid of his superiors, who were like the aggressive father he had had to endure as a boy. His own reasons for leaving his employment, therefore, were not the real reasons; they were *rationalisations* of his emotional need to avoid his problems. It follows that for our mental health's sake *it is important for us to be sure that all our beliefs and*

107

actions are, as far as ever possible, based upon naked truth and not upon our emotional needs.

At least one mechanism of the mind, that of *association,* is actually not a result but a cause of distress. The simplest, everyday example of this mental technique is that if one found a person, named Wendy for example, to be attractive, then for the rest of their lives that person would like the name, and start off by feeling well disposed toward all "Wendys" because in their minds, the name is associated with a good and lovely character.

Understanding the law of association can sometimes be of real importance for mental health. This happened in my own life when I constantly felt extremely depressed and had a real battle with fear whenever I returned to a certain house in Hull, Yorkshire, the city of my birth. Eventually, God helped me to see that this was not the result of the house being haunted or unpleasant in itself, but because it was very strongly associated in my mind with my years of mental illness, and so immediately when I went into it, all my symptoms automatically began to return. Once the truth had been revealed to me, my memories were healed and I was free to come and go to the house as I pleased.

The way out of many dilemmas is for us always to stop and analyse why it is that certain people, places or situations throw us into fear, confusion or panic. We must ask ourselves with what, or whom, they are associated in our past experience. If we take this problem to God, He will uncover and heal the painful memory, so it can no longer hurt us.

Another mechanism of the mind must be understood for our mental health's sake. This is known as the *law of reversed effort.* In short, this means that if in the realm of the mind we try too hard to succeed by our own efforts, then we shall automatically fail. Once again we can see this in the everyday situation when we try hard to remember someone's name. Sometimes the very effort of trying to remember causes a blockage and gets in the way of success. If we relax and stop trying to recollect the name, up it pops! Another example of this law is seen in that most of us can easily walk along a narrow path, if there isn't much that is at stake in doing so. However, if the path should happen to be a narrow ledge on a mountain-side, then our intense efforts, motivated by fear, might well lead us to fall down the precipice.

We have seen this law in operation as people suffering from insomnia find that it is the very effort of *trying* to go to sleep that actually keeps them awake! It is only when they reach the state of not caring whether or not they go to sleep that they drop into peaceful slumber.

In previous chapters I urged sufferers to fight their fears and really put their will into getting better. However, now we see how very important it is that this action is based not solely upon our own efforts but upon *faith in God.* Faith means trust, and trust means that while making our own right efforts we are at the same time relaxed in the confidence that God will bring to pass the end that we desire. So, as the Bible teaches, faith is the opposite to works or efforts (Eph. 2:8) and yet faith without works (belief not backed up by action) is dead (see James 2:17-20). Understanding this mechanism of the mind helps us to realise that we must pursue the path of mental health in a state of *relaxed concentration,* going on step by step with God into a richer, fuller life.

Finally, for our mental health's sake, it is of paramount importance that *we watch the direction in which our will is set.* In this connection, Jesus once asked a man who had been unable to walk for thirty-eight years whether or not he really wanted to be well (John 5:6). Most of us would have taken this for granted, especially as it had obviously involved tremendous efforts for this man to get to a pool which was famous for its occasional miracles of healing. Under these circumstances it would seem, on the surface, that Jesus' question to him, "Do you want to be healed?" were wasted words.

However, Jesus was acquainted with the mechanisms of the mind and was well aware that a person could be asking for healing with the conscious area of his mind, and yet basically still be finding a lot of emotional consolation in being ill. Like this man, sufferers from emotional illness must face the fact that they may unconsciously be clinging to their illness; painful as it is, it protects them from the challenge of having to live full, whole and healthy lives.

An example concerns J, a young married woman in a chronic state of anxiety who asked for my help. She was rapidly becoming a mental invalid. I eventually discovered that her life had been one of continual rejection by people close to her, and so, after she married she became fearful that she would suffer the same fate at the hands of her husband. Consequently, her subconscious mind produced an emotional illness, which provided her with a legitimate excuse to call upon her husband for special attention at any time of day or night. Further, all her other friendships had also been formed on the basis of her need for help, and she was frightened that once she declared herself to be well, then no one would want her. Eventually, she became well enough to keep people from giving up on her, but never quite well enough to be free of her need of attention. Jesus would have probed into the depths of *her will* and asked her, "Do you really *want* to be well?"

In other cases, I have known "demon-possessed" people to subconsciously cling to the last vestiges of their condition because they feared losing the constant attention of their pastor and the security they have found in the constant attention of church members.

Another lady who eventually saw that she was clinging to her neurosis gained enough insight to write the following:

"I Do Feel Ill!"

I'm ill, I'm ill—I feel "real bad"
Oh, love *me* now, I am so sad!
Lay down *your* interests, and your fun,
For "woe is *me*"—*I* feel "undone."

Focus your caring on *my* need
No other toil, nor business heed.
Just pander to *my* fainting soul
And pray to God, to make *me* whole.

Well, ... "whole" enough, to suffer less,
But not quite free from my distress!
For symptoms few, just here, and there,
Will guarantee your love and care.

Not full deliverance, yet, I ask;
For illness frees from many a task!
An "invalid" needs "special care"
While "healthy ones" must do their share!

O lower nature, with your schemes,
Forsake your self-protecting dreams;
And trust the Lord to make you whole,
And more than satisfy your soul.

Would God heal, then let you down
In trials of life, to sink, and drown?
Not He ... His power is infinite
He will uphold, with love, and might.

O inner-self, rejection fearing,
May this word your heart be cheering;
Let go the fears—fling wide the "gates",
God's love will more than compensate.

We must always realise that the mental mechanism by which the sufferer wants to maintain some measure of sickness on which to lean or by which to gain attention from others is entirely subconscious, caused by inner forces beyond the patient's knowledge. Such patients are usually entirely unaware of what they are doing. However, once they have got over their defensive anger at the uncovering of their self-deceit, they can, with God's help, really begin to come through to maturity and health. These folk need help to be convinced that they don't need their sickness and they are pleasant, lovable and acceptable in themselves. Once they really want to be well with all of their being and they have determinedly set their faces towards complete recovery, whatever the cost, then they will be in a position to discover the same healing power of God in their minds as the man at the pool of Bethesda found for his body. They too will be able to tell everyone that Jesus heals today, because they now know it to be true from their own, personal experience!

15 SURPRISED BY JOY*

Conversion to Christ is the process by which a self divided and distraught becomes united, integrated and happy under the impetus of a dynamic religious experience. This was certainly true in my own experience, and I also had the privilege of seeing the same process take place in the lives of hundreds of people to whom I have since ministered. It has been the reality of a deep relationship with God which has brought wholeness to their minds and emotions.

A typical example is that of J.T., a woman in her mid-thirties who lives at Waltham Abbey, Hertfordshire, England. She described her experience as follows:

> "My nerves and agoraphobia started when I was nineteen. I spent most of my days sitting on a chair holding on to a fireguard scared even to walk across the room. I came to the Lord about three years ago. Isn't it a lovely thought to know that Jesus accepts us for what we are and then remoulds us. What a friend!
>
> "Well, I decided that after fourteen years of treatment I no longer needed a psychiatrist, because I have the promise that Jesus will make me well. So last week I went to my hospital therapy group and said that I didn't need to come any more. The psychologist knew that I had been receiving divine healing, and gave me half an hour to tell the group about it.
>
> "In difficult times I listen to tapes and have a really good chat with the Lord and find real peace in Him."

---

* The title of a book by Professor C.S. Lewis in which he described his conversion experience.

Another lady who testified to the healing power of encountering the Risen Jesus said, "I had been suffering from severe depression for twelve months, but I am glad to say that since I met Jesus, I gradually improved and after about ten days the depression disappeared!"

It can be stated without doubt that a real experience of God in Jesus Christ is the greatest force for wholeness and integration of the personality this side of eternity. It is a source of incredible peace, joy and happiness.

Such an experience, however, must not be confused with mere *churchianity* or "institutional Christianity" with its creeds, rituals, traditions, and acts of worship which, although good in themselves, do not necessarily communicate God to the human heart. Seekers after God must penetrate beyond such church ordinances to a real, vital and genuine experience with our heavenly Father. He is a living, caring all-powerful Person who longs to *saturate* those who come to Him with His love, the source of all true life, joy and peace.

Jesus once said that this entrance into deep life with God is like a second birth, which, unlike the first, natural one, can only be brought about by the Holy Spirit. He told Nicodemus, a ruler of the Jews, a very religious, devout, good-living and sincere man, that even he needed to be born again (John 3:5-7). What did Jesus mean by this expression?

Jesus was drawing an analogy between physical and spiritual birth and pointing out that just as there is a natural world all around an unborn child, so there is also very close to each one of us a spiritual one called the kingdom of God. It is the world of God's love, beauty, peace, joy, holiness and power. It is peopled with angels, archangels, and all the company of heaven.* Jesus was explaining that although it is the realm of eternity, it is also possible for human beings

*See the Church of England's order for the service of Holy Communion.

114

to begin to experience it now, by undergoing a process of *spiritual* birth by being "born from above", by the miraculous work of the Holy Spirit. From the moment this miracle takes place, Jesus said, one can *begin to experience* the realities of the kingdom of God in just as real and vital a way as the realities of the physical world can be sensed and enjoyed. St Paul later affirmed that those who have been born again by the Holy Spirit are brand new people. For them, "old things are passed away; behold, all things are become new" (2 Cor. 5:17 KJV).

It must be remembered, however, that just as a newborn's first experience of the world is very limited and only gradually becomes more complete, so a newly born Christian's knowledge of the realities of the kingdom of God will always be a slow, but ever-increasing, process of development.

The Bible is an inspired record of just what genuine experience of God should be like, and it enumerates many blessings that flow from knowing our heavenly Father. For instance, it describes conversion as a very liberating experience in the words, "If the Son makes you free, you will be free indeed" (John 8:36). It draws a parallel between Christian freedom and that of a life-long slave who, suddenly discovering he is a free man because he has been redeemed (1 Pet. 2:18-19), begins to seek God and plan his new, free life with intense excitement! So, too, God's born-again children can know and feel that they have been set free from bondage to guilt, fear, depression and all other works of the Enemy (2 Tim. 4:18). As they accept this freedom as a fact which God has accomplished for them, they flex their muscles and find that the chains have fallen off. They walk through the door that has imprisoned their hearts and minds into a new and wonderful life.

St Paul also uses the language of the court of law to indicate the fact that all Christians are completely acquitted by God from all the sins we have ever committed, because Jesus His Son has paid the price for us. St Paul explains that He did this for all of us by dying upon the Cross, thereby releasing us from the penalty we have incurred by our sins as we stand before the judgment seat of God. So, when we realise this to be true, our joy and relief is like that of a criminal who suddenly finds he is no longer under a sentence of death, but is free to go home and live a new life.

We Christians should also realise that God has adopted us into His family and has given us a tremendous, incalculable spiritual *inheritance* which is ours by legal right, as heirs of the Father and joint heirs with His Son Jesus Christ (Rom. 8:14-17). This means that all the blessings of heaven are ours *now* (Eph. 1:3). We are now sharers in all God's riches of love, joy, peace and health. Paul promises that "My God will supply every need of yours according to his riches in glory in Christ Jesus" (Phil. 4:19). So we no longer have any need to be anxious about anything!

Within the community of faith, we are called upon to exercise a *rightful discipline in every aspect of our lives.* We need not be subject to all sorts of petty rules and regulations, but we do learn what it means to receive a spirit of discipline and of a sound mind (see 2 Tim. 1:7). Despite the inevitable imperfections of the Church, we should be led by God's Spirit into an increasingly balanced and healthy life.

We Christians seek to live out a new quality of life, not because we have to but because as God's children, we really want to! God gives us, His children, a new course and direction of wholeness. This is the Jesus-directed life, through which God imparts all the gifts and graces of His own beautiful life of peace, so that believers can face the many harsh realities of life with a new hope and a true optimism, based on the fact that this is God's world, and the final issues of every human life, including their own, are in His hands (Ps. 31:15; Job 14:5).

Deeply committed Christians also learn another important lesson vital to mental health. This is that emotionally sick people are far too introspective, tense and self-centred. Part of their illness is that the whole of their world revolves around themselves, their own needs and their own problems. However, a real experience of God changes all this. Christians share God's love with others and see life from God's point of view. For this reason they begin to be much more aware of the needs of others and much more thankful for their own blessings. They begin to lose their obsession with self and life takes an outward direction as they help and serve other people. They *become outward bound,* always looking for some occupation in which to be usefully engaged and some service to perform for the Lord who has saved them.

In this new dimension of living, born-again Christians discover the answer to that vital question, *"Who am I?"* They know that they are each a child chosen by God. They also know why they are here in the world: *to know and serve Him for ever* (Isa. 43:21).

Further, they know where they are going ultimately because from their own inner being they have the sure conviction that they are journeying to heaven (Heb. 13:14). They begin to view life's difficulties, temptations, trials and problems in the light of eternity, and will see that, as they react to them positively, God will use them as material for making them more and more into that beautiful person it is your destiny to be (Heb. 12:11).

We Christians are happier, more fulfilled, peaceful, rested and more mature people as a result of our relationship with God and His people. Our relationships, home life, daily work, and community service are richer, fuller, more positive and more effective as we pray, wait

117

upon God, seek wise counsel and live a secure wholesome life. As the Church of England prayer book puts it, "Amidst all the changes and chances of this transitory life, our hearts will truly there be fixed, where true joys will be found."

And nothing will be able to separate us from the love of God which is in Christ Jesus your Lord—nothing in the past, present or future—nothing in all creation, NOT EVEN DEATH (Rom. 8:38).

APPENDIX 1

A Testimony from Esther

For months on end, I sat fearfully huddled in a small room in my home, locked in by my husband, at my *request*. All day I sat there alone, in solitary confinement. This was because my mind was obsessed with terrible fears that everything I said and did would cause harm and destruction to others. If I ever tried to come out of the room, then inner voices would plague me, suggesting the many ways in which I might somehow accidentally cause harm to others. My mind was perpetually filled with horrible visions of accidents and dreadful incidents I might cause to happen. Only by having myself locked safely away could I silence these accusing voices by asserting, "I've been locked in all day, I couldn't possibly have hurt anyone." This was the only measure of peace I could find, but even then it was a very troubled form of peace, fraught with tension and horror.

I would only move from my locked room if somebody accompanied me, watching me all the time. I was obsessed with making detailed notes of all that I did in my life. My husband, parents and friends supported me wonderfully all through my illness, yet at one point my fears grew so bad that I even dreaded speaking to my mother in case my words would harmfully misguide her. The terror I felt when confronted by complete strangers was much worse.

Every day was unbearable, and nights were equally tormented. In order to sleep, I had to tour round and round the house checking that all was well with doors and gas taps, etc., and then ask my husband to lock us both in the bedroom and hang the key around his neck. On bad nights, I even used to tie my wrist to the bedpost, in order to find some sense of security.

Eventually, I spent two months in a psychiatric hospital but was finally discharged because the doctor said that the hospital environment was only worsening my condition. For some years, I continued to be treated by different doctors and psychiatrists, each one trying out a different form of treatment on me. They did help me by explaining the mental process whereby I had become so troubled, but none of them seemed to be able to show me the way out of this terrible bondage. So I remained in my locked room.

Before this illness took hold of me, I had lived a full and busy life as a housewife and school teacher. I had become a Christian at the age of sixteen and had been much involved in church activities. But, although I was comforted in my illness by the knowledge that God loved me and was with me, I somehow seemed to be utterly unable to release my faith to help myself out of my illness. Well-meaning exhortations from other Christians to "have more faith in God" only drove me deeper into despair and guilt, because I was just not able to bring my tormented fantasies into control. There seemed to be no answer anywhere in the world.

Eventually, however, I discovered that God is far, far greater than the greatest problem. I read in my Bible that Jesus came to be a light to those who sit in darkness and in the shadow of death and to guide our feet into the way of peace (Luke 1:79). For the dispersing of my own particular darkness I needed to learn the lesson of Peter when he walked upon the water, that is to take my eyes off the tumultuous waves of fear, and fix them instead upon Jesus and His power, and constantly declare His victory over the situation.

I have discovered the Lord to be gracious and a patient

teacher. He brought me out of that locked room and step by step caused me to be able to do more and more normal activities alone, like moving freely around my own home, going into the garden, wandering down the street, visiting a friend nine miles away, attending church, being able to stay in the house for several nights for a stretch with Jesus alone as my keeper. How I treasure this ever-growing liberty. I can even rejoice at such a simple activity as the sheer delight of being able to stand alone in the kitchen and peel potatoes!

Gradually, God has given me the confidence to be involved with more and more people. At one time I wanted the phone to be locked away, in case I made uncontrollable calls that would cause chaos and injury to others, but I now use it frequently in my work. Once I could not even make myself a cup of coffee; now I am able to hold fellowship meetings in my home. Once I was fearful of even speaking to my mother, but now God has enabled me to speak at children's meetings and to visit various churches to speak of my experience of His love.

Five minutes in a car used to be a strain, yet now the Lord has made me able to enjoy five hundred miles passenger travel in ten days. I can delight in holidays at conference centres, mixing happily with strangers.

For years, without God's strength or the deep inner knowledge of His upholding power and love, I could do nothing but cringe away from life in the depths of fear and depression. But, as the Scriptures say, "With God, nothing shall be impossible", and I have experienced this in amazing ways as God has reversed my impossible situations, and made nightmare circumstances into times of victory and praise.

It has not been a speedy journey, but it has been a steady one as every day I have learned how to enter deeper into the inner knowledge of God's love and keeping power.

The tide of my illness began to turn as I entered into a dual ministry of (a) receiving prayer, with the laying on of hands, and (b) learning how to meditate deeply upon the Word of God. Through the prayer ministry, the Holy Spirit was able to begin a healing work in those deep inner places of the soul where all the confusion had its roots. Through meditation upon Jesus and His loving power, my confidence in Him grew, and this prepared me for the next step along the pathway, laying hold of the promises of God, by faith and in His strength, and beginning to let go of my false securities such as the locked room.

Just as a baby learns to toddle and often stumbles and falls, so I too have faltered frequently in my attempts to journey into wholeness. In fact, I still have quite a few fears to overcome and I need continually to rest upon God's Word. Yet, gradually, the Lord is drawing me on to reclaim the life of which I was so terribly robbed by illness.

I have found the journey back to health also to be a real battle because the Enemy does not like to let his prisoners go! However, often he cannot resist the power of God, and Trevor Dearing taught me to ward off the fears of my own harmfulness by quoting and living the Word of God, His precious promises to me. I like to sum up the whole of my testimony in the following words.

> No hope, no joy—deep dark despair,
> Shut in a room, just sitting there.
> Day after day, with no respite,
> Longing for death to end my plight.
> Fear upon fear, tormenting my soul,
> "Why, O Lord, why, don't you make me whole?"
> "Trust Me, My child, I'll bring you release,
> Teach you to walk in the paths of peace:
> Study My Word, and delight in Me,
> For *knowing* your Lord will set you free.

Launch out in faith, one step at a time;
Thus, out of darkness, you'll surely climb."
Praise God! He performed all He said,
Delivered my soul from its dread;
Caused me to see His love and His power;
Taught me to trust Him, throughout each hour;
Lifted me up from depths of despair,
And made me secure in His tender care.

So as I continue to follow the advice given in this book, and also build on the lessons I have learned myself, I approach the remaining hurdles along this journey into peace with confidence, *knowing* that God, who has begun a good work in me, will fulfil His promise to bring it to a wonderful conclusion to His glory (Phil. 1:6). Praise Him for all His works. I no longer need drugs and have no medical help. My trust is in the living Lord Jesus Christ himself, whom I know from my own experience to be the Greatest Physician of all!

APPENDIX 2

Healing By Meditation

Whenever you feel ill, fearful or depressed, then set aside fifteen minutes every day for the following exercise. Make sure that you go into a private room where you can shut yourself in alone with God, without any fear of interruption (Matt. 6:6). Remember God sees in secret and meets you in the secret place in your heart.

Sit or lie down; relax your body, but concentrate your mind on God. Remember that He is very near. Dwell on one of these scriptural sentences, first learning it by heart, repeating it aloud several times. Then go over it repeatedly, emphasising and thinking about the meaning of a *different* word every time, applying the test to yourself.

For example, take Philippians 4:13: "I *can do all* things in him [Jesus] who strengthens me." First *learn* the sentence by heart, then reflect on it again, confessing that I can do all things through Christ who strengthens me. In the next session emphasise the word *can* then the word *all*. Eventually begin to absorb the fact that this promise is true, through Christ who *strengthens me.* Finally absorb and inwardly digest the whole sentence. Use this text for several days or whenever you feel inadequate, weak, or face a task which makes you afraid. Remember that it is God's living Word. It will be a source of power, effecting that which it promises in your life.

Other texts I suggest for us to use in this way are:

Isa. 26:3 Thou dost keep him in perfect peace, whose mind is stayed on thee, because he trusts in thee.

Isa. 40:31 I will wait upon the Lord and He will renew my strength. I shall mount up with wings as an eagle. I shall run and not be weary, walk and not faint.

Jude 24 Now to Him who is able to keep me from falling and to present me without blemish before the presence of His glory with rejoicing be glory, praise, and honour.

Phil. 4:19 My God will supply every need of mine according to His riches in glory in Christ Jesus.

Ps. 18:6, 16-17, 19 In my distress I will call upon the Lord; to my God I cry for help. He reaches from on high, He takes me, He draws me out of many waters. He delivers me from my strong enemy and from those who hate me. He brings me forth into a broad place; He delivers me, because He delights in me.

Ps. 34:7 The Angel of the Lord encamps around me and delivers me.

Ps. 40:1-2 I waited patiently for the Lord; He inclines to me and hears my cry. He draws me up from the desolate pit, out of the miry bog, and sets my feet upon a rock, making my steps secure.

John 5:18 I know that I am a true child of God, in the charge of God's only Son, and the evil one keeps his distance.

Ps. 31:8 He has not abandoned me to the power of the enemy, but has set me free.

2 Tim. 1:7 God did not give me a spirit of fear, but a spirit of power and love and self-control.

Matt. 11:28 Jesus said, "Come to me, all who labour and are heavy laden, and I will give you rest. Take my yoke upon you and learn from me; for I am gentle and lowly in heart and you will find rest for your souls."

Ps. 91:15 When I call upon God, He will answer me, and be with me in trouble, and will rescue me.

1 Pet. 5:7 I cast all my care upon Him, because He cares for me.

Deut. 33:27 The eternal God is my refuge and underneath are His everlasting arms.

Eph. 3:20 He is able to do far more abundantly above all that I ask or think according to the power at work within me.

Ps. 91:10 There shall no evil come near me. No plague shall come near my dwelling.

Isa. 49:15-16 God will not forget me for He has engraven me on the palms of His hands; and my walls are continually before Him.

Isa. 54:10 His steadfast love shall not depart from me, and His covenant of peace shall not be removed, says the Lord who has compassion on me.

John 14:27 His peace He leaves with me; His peace He gives to me; not as the world gives does He give to me. My heart will not be troubled, neither will I be afraid.

Jer. 31:3 He has loved me with an everlasting love, and has continued His faithfulness to me.

Luke 12:6, 7 Even the hairs of my head are all numbered by my Father. I will not fear.

Matt. 28:20 He is with me always, to the close of the age.

Isa. 41:10 I will not fear, for He is with me; I will not be dismayed, for He is my God and He will strengthen me. He will help me; He will uphold me with His victorious right hand.

Ps. 91:15 When I call upon God, He will answer me, and be with me in trouble, and will rescue me.

Isa. 43:1, 2 God has redeemed me and has called me by my name. I am His. When I pass through the waters He is with me, and through the rivers, they shall not overwhelm me.

Search the Scriptures yourself, and you will find many more living promises from God, tailor-made to meet your needs! Always finish by thanking God that His word is true for you.